Quasimodo von Belvedere
Independent Superman of Chicago

Trevor Blake, Editor

mogtus-sanlux
Knoxville 2026

Quasimodo von Belvedere: Independent Superman of Chicago
by Trevor Blake (editor)
Copyright © 2026 Trevor Blake
"Family Stories" Copyright © 2026 by Chloris W. Noelke-Olson
All rights reserved.

Cover Design by Kevin I. Slaughter

First Impression: January 2026
Knoxville: mogtus-sanlux

Blake, Trevor
[English]
Quasimodo von Belvedere: Independent Superman of Chicago
ISBN 978-1-944651-37-4
1. Chicago
2. Biography
Trevor Blake (b. 1966); Quasimodo von Belvedere (Eternity - Forever)

mogtus-sanlux 400
Stand Alone 1317

> "A procession of the damned. By the damned, I mean the excluded. We shall have a procession of data that Science has excluded. Battalions of the accursed, captained by pallid data that I have exhumed, will march. You'll read them — or they'll march. Some of them livid and some of them fiery and some of them rotten."
>
> — Charles Fort, *The Book of the Damned* (1919)

mogtus-sanlux.one
~mogtus-sanlux

127 House: At every turn in its thought society will find us waiting.

Table of Contents

Introduction 1

The Mutterings of a Lobster 7
   The Volcano of Genius 9
   A Clever Satire 9
   The Progressive Lobster 9
   Genius, Interrupted 10
   To Avert Future Wars 10
   European War as the Most Vital Factor 12
   Why the Doom of Predatory Civilization Cannot Be Averted ... 15

Hollow Point 17
   The Conscience of a Dum-Dum Bullet Chapter 1 19
   The Conscience of a Dum-Dum Bullet Chapter 2 23
   The Conscience of a Dum-Dum Bullet Chapter 3 27
   The Conscience of a Dum-Dum Bullet Chapter 4 33
   The Conscience of a Dum-Dum Bullet Chapter 5 37
   The Conscience of a Dum-Dum Bullet Chapter 6 41
   The Conscience of a Dum-Dum Bullet Chapter 7 47
   The Conscience of a Dum-Dum Bullet Chapter 8 51

Your Next President 57
   Hon. Quasimodo von Belvedere is Criticizing the Government .. 59
   Nomination Speech 61
   Campaign Speech 69
   My Nearest Approach to Death 73
   Two Pickles, a Rabbi and a Bishop 76
   The History of a Pig and a Sack of Potatoes 77
   Asks for Vamp, One Qualifies, Then He... 83
   "Pup Kafe No Place for Lady," Says Florence 84
   House of Correction Patrons May Be Right 85
   A Health Recipe 85
   The Moustache of Quasimodo von Belvedere 86

A Frightfulness of the Past 89
   Family Stories 91

Sources 109

Your Introduction to Quasimodo von Belvedere: Independent Superman

by Trevor Blake

QUASIMODO von Belvedere was born in the early 1900s in Chicago, Illinois. He was an author and a social commentator. He was a little-known candidate for President of the United States of America, running on the "more or less Progressive Ticket of the Independent Superman Element." Gathered here for the first time is the more or less complete story of his life and work.

It is natural that von Belvedere would gravitate toward the bohemian city of Chicago, for reasons that will be revealed soon enough. Life in bohemian Chicago wasn't easy, but it was free — free in the sense of "stop me if you can." Vagrants ran the Hotel de Gink chain of work-to-rent hotels. The line between organized crime and the police force had never been more thin, which served underground clubs well as long as the protection money stayed paid. Intellectual pursuits were not limited to an intellectual clique, and instead "hobo colleges" were in session. Most welcoming of all for the independent superman, free speech was as free as it gets. Public meetings in Washington Square Park were free for the speaking and hearing. The Dil Pickle Club[1] and, later, the House of Blazes, were free speech havens. The truth or morality of the speech was less important than the monomania of the speaker. As light is drawn to the moth, Quasimodo von Belvedere was drawn to Chicago.

In Chicago, some mounted the speaker's soapbox in Washington Square Park, while others kept their quiet smile off to the side. And some did more than speak. First among those who joined deed to work is the Industrial Workers of the World. We do well to learn why Quasimodo von Belevedere gave the high praise to the I. W. W. to be found in this volume.

The Industrial Workers of the World is an international organization founded in 1905 in Chicago, Illinois. The Preamble to their Guiding Principles and Rules is little changed since that time:

---

[1] Both "Dil Pickle Club" and "Dill Pickle Club," with one or two ls in the first word, are found in the historic record. Because the single-l spelling was painted above the entrance to the 'Pickle itself, this is our preferred spelling.

The working class and the employing class have nothing in common. There can be no peace so long as hunger and want are found among millions of the working people and the few, who make up the employing class, have all the good things of life. Between these two classes a struggle must go on until the workers of the world organize as a class, take possession of the means of production, abolish the wage system, and live in harmony with the earth.

A member of the I.W.W. demands a simple alternative to the daydreams of anarchists, communists, socialists, priest and reformers.

The Industrial Workers of the World took on the nickname the "Wobblies" when a man for whom English was not a native language attempted to say aloud their abbreviation. He pronounced I. W. W. as "eye-wobble-wobble."

Since their founding, the Wobblies have improved the working conditions in many factories, shops, mines and other worksites all across the world. In their struggle to achieve their goals, hundreds of Wobblies have been fired, blacklisted, tortured, imprisoned and lynched. They published dozens of newspapers, magazines books and have a website.[1]

---
[1] iww.org

The I. W. W. exists today. Find a branch near you, read their tremendous back catalog of publications and find out more about this significant and fascinating organization, the "One Big Union."

The Wobblies of a century ago took pains to differentiate themselves from both the left and the right. They mocked (and sometimes fought) both communists and the Ku Klux Klan. In advocating for industrial organization they refrained from unionizing any individual shop or industry.

As Quasimodo von Belvedere was an enthusiast for the I. W. W., the Wobblies were enthusiastic distributors of the book *Might is Right* by Ragnar Redbeard. Born Arthur Desmond, the author of *Might is Right* made his living as an ice cream vendor until he defended the business from the police with a Boer-war rifle. He opened a mail-order book business, variously called Thurland & Thurland or The House o' Gowrie. He lived in Chicago during the time of both Quasimodo von Belvedere and the I. W. W. In the undated first issue of *The Dil Pickler*, edited by Dil Pickle founder Jack Jones, there is a (imaginary) list of books donated to the 'Pickle by The House o' Gowrie, and one of them is "English As Is" by Vincent Nogi — one of many variant spellings of the man who was Quasimodo von Belvedere. The *braggadocio* of the Independent Superman is likely a friendly mockery of the egoist undercurrent found in the "hobohemia" of Chicago.

Fraternal harmony among the Picklers was not undisturbed. Jack Jones sought a patent for a wooden pull-toy he called the Du-Dil-Duk. Vincent Noga claimed Jones stole the idea, according to *The Damnedest Radical* by Roger A. Bruns.[1]

If there was a center for the eccentrics of Chicago a century ago, it was the Dil Pickle Club. Jack Jones, the owner, was a Wobbly. The Dil Pickle Club published an edition of Ragnar Redbeard's book *Might is Right*. The Dil Pickle Club was located in Tooker Alley, next to Washington Square Park — or, as Quasimodo von Belvendere refers to it, Trotzky Square. von Belvedere also makes reference to the nearby Newberry Library and the Radical Bookshop. Above the entrance to the Dil Pickle Club was the legend "Step High, Stoop Low and Leave Your Dignity Outside." Interracial dances, sex lecturers, political speakers (heretical only), amateur dramas — as long as it courted controversy, you could find it at the 'Pickle. They kept the lights on (if dimly) throughout many years of ill repute but eventually Jones refused to pay the protection money required by the local police. Soon after the club was closed forever.

---

[1] Urbana: University of Illinois Press, 1986. p. 237.

But you don't get rid of a bunch of oddballs just by closing down one of their venues. The 'Pickle alumni went on to form the House of Blazes, and it was in the House of Blazes that Quasimodo von Belvedere delivered some of his finest orations (at least on paper). And when even the House of Blazes was extinguished, our hero founded the House of Corrections to insure a skirting of custom and law would continue.

As a candidate for President on the Independent Superman ticket, Quasimodo von Belvedere was a keen student of his competition. He kept a good eye on the 1901 to 1909 administration of Theodore Roosevelt and the 1913 to 1921 administration of Woodrow Wilson, with particular emphasis on their treatment of the working man and their readiness to send the United States to war. von Belvedere was free with his insights into World War I and Wilson's Fourteen Point plan to exit the war he had entered. von Belvedere saw the changes that came from the Russian Revolution of 1917, the creation of the League of Nations, and the burden of suffrage to women in the United States. The years of Prohibition (1920 - 1933) saw Quasimodo von Belvedere escorted from his own House of Corrections to the State's House of Corrections. He kept his eye on the world, and the world (or at least this book) now turns its eye to him.

—

THE SUPERMAN

Chronology tempts the reader to sort Superman as a term and a concept in a linear fashion. But we each get the Superman we want, informed incompletely from the rest across time and introduced in parody as much as in philosophy. The lives of the heralds of Superman are often at odds with the Superman himself.

The idea that some men are Great Men has no origin outside the origin of the species. All people in all places have observed this basic fact, and only in our modern age do we pretend otherwise. It was obvious to our ignorant and savage ancestors that there are men and there are Supermen. Supermen were born that way, or made themselves so, or were favored / cursed by the gods, and that was that. There are no ancient texts about Superman-ness.

The Industrial Revolution of the mid-1800s was something new under the sun: a meat grinder that could pulp the Great and common man alike into a sausage fit for a politician. It was the Industrial Revolution which caused some authors to talk about the Superman as a type, because they could see he was being fed into a mechanism which would render him indistinguishable from other men. That mechanism, the alien, a-human machine was called "equality."

For the early heralds of the Superman one may read the "Hero Lectures" of Thomas Carlyle (1840), *Der Einzige und sein Eigentum* (*The Ego and His Own*) by Max Stirner (1845), "Representative Men" by Ralph Waldo Emerson (1850), and other texts. These works do not use the exact word Superman but the idea is there.

The dawn of the Superman by the name Superman comes in 1883 with *Also sprach Zarathustra: Ein Buch für Alle und Keinen* (Thus Spoke Zarathustra: A Book for All and None) by Friedrich Nietzsche (1883 - 1885). Here is a key passage:

> Ich lehre euch den Übermenschen. Der Mensch ist Etwas, das überwunden werden soll. Was habt ihr getan, ihn zu überwinden?

In 1909, this passage was translated by Thomas Common as:

> I teach you the Superman. Man is something to be surpassed. What have ye done to surpass man?

Common was among the first, if not the first, translators of Nietzsche into English. Nietzsche's sister chose other men to be her brother's sanctioned translators. These later translators favored the word of "Overman" instead of "Superman," but Superman came first. As he should!

Nietzsche may or may not have read Stirner, but George Bernard Shaw definitely read Nietzsche. Shaw's 1899 play "Man and Superman" may have influenced Common when he translated *Übermensch* as "Superman." The third act of the play is titled "Don Juan in Hell" and includes this exchange between The Devil and a statue of Don Gonzalo, who was the father of Doña Ana, who was a shade of Ann Whitefield, a lead character in the first two acts:

> THE STATUE. And who the deuce is the Superman?
> THE DEVIL. Oh, the latest fashion among the Life Force fanatics. Did you not meet in Heaven, among the new arrivals, that German Polish madman — what was his name? Nietzsche?
> THE STATUE. Never heard of him.
> THE DEVIL. Well, he came here first, before he recovered his wits. I had some hopes of him; but he was a confirmed Life Force worshipper. It was he who raked up the Superman, who is as old as Prometheus; and the twentieth century will run after this newest of the

> old crazes when it gets tired of the world, the flesh, and your humble servant.
>
> THE STATUE. Superman is a good cry; and a good cry is half the battle. I should like to see this Nietzsche.

Nietzsche wrote of the *Übermensch*, Shaw wrote of Nietzsche writing of the Superman, and Common translated Nietzsche's *Übermensch* as Superman.

Stanisław Szukalski (1893 - 1987) was a philosopher disguised as a sculptor and artist. He was born in Poland and emigrated to the United States. Like Quasimodo von Belvedere, he gravitated to the bohemia of Chicago. In fact, his studio for a time was located in Tooker Alley, steps away from the Dil Pickle Club. It is highly likely that these two crossed paths. It is therefore of note that in a 1928 poster titled "The Parade of the Chicago Artists to the No-Jury Artists Cubist Ball" dated 1928 and executed by Emil Armin, Szukalski is described as "The self-confessed Michigan Avenue Superman."

The Independent Superman of Quasimodo von Belvedere strides among mere mortals in the light of Carlyle, Stirner, Emerson, Nietzsche, Common, Redbeard and others. He may or may not have read them, but they were in the air. They were in the air because the men who were habituates of the Dil Pickle Club like Szukalski and Redbeard had, most definitely, read them. Men talk, whispers of the Superman and his coming were about. He comes... tomorrow.

And it is as the Man of Tomorrow, in Chicago, the City of Tomorrow, that we today best know Superman. Jerry Siegel and Joe Shuster, both age nineteen, wrote a short story about a fictional character of terrible power in a 1933 comic named "The Reign of the Superman." Their Superman was a villain, and they were unable to sell the story to a publisher. They kept the name, recast the villain to a hero, switched from short story to comic strip, expanded from comic strip to comic book, and in 1938 National Allied Publications (later DC) published the first issue of *Action Comics* featuring — Superman! Hero of Metropolis, the City of Tomorrow made from equal parts of Fritz Lang's 1927 film of the same name and the Century of Progress World's Fair in Chicago, Illinois, 1933.

The Mutterings of a Lobster

by Trevor Blake

HERE gathered for the first time are the earliest published works by and about Quasimodo von Belvedere.

The Volcano of Genius is a lost work by Quasimodo von Belvedere. What is printed here is all known information on the booklet in the hopes that someone, somewhere will have a copy. The volcanic nature of the genius is revealed in a few brief words about *The Mutterings of a Lobster*, another lost work earlier known as *The Progressive Lobster*. Three items on the imminent Great War follow, each revealing small details of a European background and outlook.

Never again will we have access to the straight facts about our hero, as found in these early works. From this point forward the facts are deliciously marbled with his fancies.

IWW: *The One Big Union Monthly* (March 1th, 1919) Vol. I No. 1

The Volcano of Genius

NOGA (Vincene)* Chicago, Ill. Volcano of Genius; or, The Progressive Lobster. 16 p. front (port.) 8vo [16100] (C) Aug. 10, 1911; 2 c. Aug. 14, 1911; A 294654.

—

A Clever Satire

A clever satire on Roosevelt is just out. It is published by Vincene Noga, 157 East Ohio Street, Chicago, Ill., and costs twenty-five cents. It is entitled, *The Progressive Lobster*.

—

The Progressive Lobster

The Progressive Lobster is an unusually clever satire on Roosevelt from the pen of Comrade Vincent Noga, His ready humor, his wonderful allegoric descriptive skill and the caustic mockery of his laugh makes this pamphlet, in spite of its modest title of a mere lobster, appear as a whale in the ocean of Socialistic literature. Single copies 25c. Liberal discounts to agents. For sale by Fred Nidrich, 2620 Seminary Ave., Chicago, III.

Genius, Interrupted in Work, Throws Water on Landlady

Vincent Noga Explains in Court He Was Writing a Novel, but Judge Proves Unsympathetic and Fines Him.

MRS. Adolph Hirt, who manages a rooming house at 31 East Illinois street, admits lack of sympathy with literary genius.

The genius — he admits it — is Vincent Noga, one of the roomers. He is writing a novel. He confessed to throwing the glass of water at Mrs. Hirt when she came to protest that his typewriting was disturbing her other lodgers.

"I'm an author," he explained. "I've written one book. It was called 'The Mutterings of a Lobster,' and was a criticism of Roosevelt. It was not a success. I think it was too good, and so now I'm writing a novel that's a wonder. Here's page twenty of it — 'These words filled her desolate soul with ineffable joy — '"

"Enough," interrupted Judge Scully. "Listen to my words, and see what effect they have on your desolate soul. 'Ten dollars and costs.'"

To Avert Future Wars

SCORES of Bohemians and Poles have recently been executed because of their lack of love for their respective kaisers.

No one familiar with the kind of treatment the Bohemians have been receiving at the hands of the Hapsburg potentates would expect them to jump into the fire for their sakes. Their fate, however, is not as adverse as that of the Prussian Poles, whose treatment is absolutely barbaric.

The Hapsburgs are merely devouring the bread of the Bohemians, while in their Germanizing mania the Hohenzollerns are snapping their teeth into the very souls of the Poles.

I am not prepared to disprove that Germanization may be beneficent to the natives of German colonies in Africa, but that it has an absolutely degrading influence upon the Poles is not open to question.

If two children of equal intelligence, one German and one Polish, are placed in the care of a German tutor, their educational opportunity becomes extremely unequal, one understanding the teacher's language and the other not. Were the Pole a budding Michiewicz he could not be transformed by Germanization any more than he could be transformed into a Bostonian by being fed on pork and beans.

The Poles have virile blood in their veins, and a greater German than their Slowacki Mickeqicz or Sinkiewicz is yet to be born. But unless they soon regain their liberty they will lose their seat upon the Olympus of culture. That Germany has anything to gain by annihilating their culture is doubtful.

Speaking of oppressors it is more proper to refer to the Hohenzollern family rather than to Germany, for the Germans as a whole are one of the most noble races on earth. My own experience has taught me how ill-founded is the hostility between the Teutonic and the Slavic nations. Being a Bohemian and having been raised in subjection under the despotic hand of a Teutonic monarch I grew up with a brazen conviction that the Slavs were angels and the Germans demons. When I emigrated to Germany I soon found myself living amid the finest people imaginable. Some of the many friends I made there admitted frankly that they did not esteem the Bohemians very highly and that I was an exception and that I should really have been a German. This suggested to me that they had as little reason for their antipathy to Slavs as the Slavs had for them.

Had I never had the opportunity to learn what the Germans really are, reading the present war news I would chuckle with savage joy that the enemies of my race were being exterminated; but since my insight into history teaches me the priceless truth that racial discords were originated and are being cultivated by individuals and not by the people, and since my intimate acquaintance with my supposed enemies and my test of their matchless hospitality, I see only abomination in punishing the German race for the domineering greed of the Hapsburgs, Bismarcks and Hohenzollerns.

This martial conflagration in Europe was kindled by the eruption of hatred of a small oppressed race, and while it may be impossible to check the present havoc, its repetition can be averted by setting the various sections of the different enthralled nations free.

European War as the Most Vital Factor in Moulding of Destiny of Our Nation

1914

THE European war will have an infinitely greater influence upon the future of United States than upon its participants. Its effect upon Europe will be only transient; the European rivers will continue to flow after the cessation of the slaughter as they did before and will carry the blood and the carcasses of the victims into the eager throat of the sea and in a few days will be digested; the soil too will assimilate its portion; gradually the wrecked cities, bridges and railroad tracks will be rehabilitated; and inasmuch as the promoters of the mischief will be unable to assimilate the source of life itself, men and beasts will reproduce and replenish the loss in a generation or two; depending on the duration of the conflict.

Should any of the the belligerent countries now blessed with a czar republicanize its government by substituting the monarch with a president, metamorphose its princes, dukes, lords, magnates, pashas, etc., into plain, sensible citizens of the order of our Achbolds, Morgans or Pattens, this transformation will be harmless in itself and of no more importance than the change of the fashion, and while it may be conceded that it had been hastened by this cataclysm it would be be absurd to consider it as its result, for hardly anyone rebuilds his house, wrecked by a storm, in the exact same pattern of the one demolished. The real causes for the deviation embodied in his new house have their roots in the evolution of his ideas, the refinements of his tastes and in the changes of his requirements, but not in the least in the storm. Should the Chicago post office be wrecked today, our government, due to the recent unprecedented expansion of the postal service, would rehabilitate it with a structure twice as large to meet the present requirements, while, in case the earth should swallow The Hague Peace Palace — now that its nugacity is so irrefragably established — that institution would be substituted with one considerably smaller, and less gorgeous, possibly an old box car if replaced at all.

Thus while the war means to Europe scarcely more than a temporary weakness or a passing headache does to an individual, it will revolutionize the manner of our existence.

It will instill a soul into our public life. The influx of foreign element into our population being checked, our people will be amalgamated into a real nation. In the course of the ensuing five years, in which period Europe will have no surplus population to discharge, our hyphenated Americans will be amalgamated into AMERICANS and astute patriots. Thus our nation will begin to exist in reality as well as upon the map. Before Europe will arise from the wreck of the recent catastrophe our population will have trebled and form thus a natural barricade against immigration.

By annihilating its navies, exterminating its armies and exhausting its vast store of ammunition, as she seems bent upon doing, Europe will transform us into an unconquerable world's power without compelling us to build a single dreadnought or even a single rifle for many years to come.

Destiny will promote us to the very Olympus of power, but to become the leading nation of the world in a moral as well as in a commercial and military sense we must cultivate more ethical integrity. Our federal administration should have spared itself from appearing ridiculous before the world by setting quietly aside one Sunday to repose from its feverish scheming to snap away the commercial fields from the belligerent nations as soon as they drown their navies than to set it aside for sham prayers for peace, which, if granted right now, in response thereto, would check our commercial aspirations. How can we hope to appear consistent even to ourselves by this "breathing hot and cold with the same breath."

Why the Doom of Predatory Civilization Cannot Be Averted

1919

SINCE the liberty of exploiting the proletariat become seriously assailed, the various civic authorities promptly set forth to silence the agitators. They jailed them; ran them down with army tanks; deported them, and even allowed the "people" to "take the law in their own hands" as a result of which "scores of wobblies went home to nurse their swollen heads and broken ribs." No sooner did we commence to rejoice over the saving of our anthropophagous democracy in our fair land than the privileged press squills frantically that, instead of diminishing, the forces of the rebels are increasing. Perceiving that the government cannot successfully cope with the situation without our advice, we immediately indited a letter to Hon. John Mitchel Palmer, offering to him practical plans as to how to rescue our civilization from the relentless teeth of the bolshevik dragon. Among several other shrewd measures we proposed that one day be set apart for a general patriotic pogrom — which shall be called LIBERTY DAY, upon which day the government would advice the people ruthlessly to take the law in their own hands, and to decimate the foreign bolshevist pest — to send its soul plumb to hell, to be nursed by the devils. The solution of the entire dark problem being so simple, we wondered why the government was waiting until we discovered it.

However, before mailing this clever letter to Mr. Palmer, we submitted it for criticism to Matys, who, in addition to being our janitor, is also our chief literary adviser. Upon a cursory perusal of our letter Matys told us bluntly that our plans were no good. He explained to us that the most exploited element in every country without distinction is the most radical one, and that in this U.S. the bulk of the most exploited element happens to be foreign born.

"The robbery perpetrated upon them," he continued, "accounts for their radicalism much better, and more logically than their foreign origin. If you kill them off, Americans shall be obliged to take their places — maybe you yourself would have to work. Subjected to the same economic adversity Americans would become equally rebellious. On the other hand, give the present rebels justice, and they will become conservative."

All this sounded so reasonable that we did not send our letter to Mr. Palmer; however, the problem remained unsolved, and this made us feel unhappy. Looking appealingly to Matys, we asked him how he would go about it to destroy Bolshevism.

"You can't destroy it," quoth he, and his voice rang with a strong emphasis. "You cannot abolish things instituted by Divine authority."

Never before did Matys speak to us with such earnestness, he astonished us. "How is that?" we cried, "do you mean to deny that Bolshevism is the product of the devil!!!"

By way of reply Matys reached for his old Bible, located the desired point and read to us: "HE WHO DOES NOT WORK SHALL NOT EAT!!!"

The One Big Union Monthly. Vol. 1 No. 3 (May 1919) p. 18.

Hollow Point

by Trevor Blake

THE dum-dum bullet was developed in Dum Dum, near Calcutta. This type of ammunition is today known as a hollow-point bullet. The hollow-point bullet expands upon contact, causing more damage to the target. For this reason, they are banned in international warfare by many nations. Some of the men who manufacture and use the dum-dum bullet may have a conscience, but the dum-dum bullet treats all men the same.

The Conscience of a Dum-Dum Bullet is a novella by Quasimodo von Belvedere. It appeared in 1919 and 1920 in *One Big Union*, a periodical produced by the Industrial Workers of the World. The current volume collects all individually chapters for the first time. This novella is a morality dialogue between Quasimodo von Belvedere, a plutocrat, and Matys, his servant with revolutionary tendencies. Like Channa leading Siddhārtha out of his palace to see the Four Sights, Matys leads his master to the slaughterhouses of Chicago. There he sees the hellish conditions described by Upton Sinclair in his 1906 novel *The Jungle*. Our hero von Belvedere is enlightened and lends his wealth and power to the revolutionary cause.

In this incarnation of Quasimodo von Belvedere, he is a Woodrow Wilson man. He reads Wilson's 1913 party platform, titled "The New Freedom." He is a capitalist with progressive tendencies, while Matys is a revolutionary prophesying the death of the current world order. Does mixing with his unwashed brethren, under an assumed funny name, with ridiculous whiskers, allow Quasimodo von Belvedere to lead his nation to peace and prosperity? Or will the tale of genius be interrupted, left for we the readers to complete? *Can Quasimodo von Belvedere, Overman, overcome the spinach* (that is, nonsense) *law*?

Read on!

The Conscience of a Dum-Dum Bullet
Chapter 1

In Which the Author Resolves to Discontinue all Tonsorial Culture of His Face; and his Forecast of the Reactionary Influence Which the Unhindered Growth of Vegetation Upon His Chin Shall Exercise Over the Coming Proletarian Civilization.

ONE murky evening when Matys (who is not only my most faithful servant, but also the most resourceful literary adviser) came to take off my boots, he made a remark that startled me. "Have you ever witnessed the dying of a man? Or an animal? An impressive spectacle," he continued after a pause, accepting my silence as attestation to my interest in the subject. "How infinitely more fascinating it must be to observe the feverish heaving and the spasmodic coughs of the expiring of an entire civilization. *There* is true Divine spectacle for you, sir!"

The *New Freedom* I was reading dropped from my hands. "Certainly I should like to see it," I cried, although I realized only a fraction of the immense import of his words.

Matys did not appear to hear me. He had my left foot in his lap and was unlacing my boot, but his mien was as grave as that of a surgeon, extirpating an appendix from the abdomen of a king. "The main artery of civilization's body had already been severed; the stench of its putrid blood is penetrating even here to the virgin forest. The end is near. A person ought to be living in some large city during these epochal developments, where he could see things. This is no time to be loafing in the woods."

"If it be so ordained that civilization perish," I said somewhat disconcertedly, extending to Matys the other foot for undressing, "by what signs shall be heralded the approaching dooms-day?"

"The signs are glaring at you already from all directions. I need indicate to you only the fundamental one, sir," said Matys, "and this symptom alone will wake you up to the fact that your civilization is mortally ill.

"Your privileged class was inoculating and fostering the opinions of the masses by the means of the school and the press, precisely after the method of your feudalistic predecessors, who held the mind of the peasantry in subjection by the means of the Church. When the feudalistic caste became so corrupt, and its Church so artificialized, as to cease to command the respect of the peasantry, the whole system fell. Now, it is obvious that the masses are becoming a trifle suspicious of your press. Do you see anything in it?"

I gasped with bewilderment at the acumen of Matys. I surely had seen something in his words. I realized in a flash that doom to the privileges of my class is impending already. If Matys himself only knew how wise he was he would not remain my servant very long. I never imagined that a meaning of such immense import could be crowed into one sentence. However, after a sober thought, much of my fright disappeared.

"It seems true enough," said I, "that our press is losing its grip upon the mind of the masses because, during the past three years, I have lost seven millions on my investments in the press. And what did I get for the seven millions? The public did the exact opposite to what my publications advocated. When I urged the acceleration of production the workers threw down their tools and went on strike. That looks to me like revolution. But cannot we captains of industry get behind the radical press and bring the revolutionists back upon the conservative path with the same chances of success as our forefathers contrived to neutralize the economic effect of Christianity by getting control of the Churches and having preached to the Christians doctrines exactly antipodal to those of Christ? You know that every Pope, as well as every Christian king, has been an anti-Christ! — Ha, ha, ha," I laughed. "I am a Bushwawiki already. Throw all my razors and all my perfumes and cosmetic powders into the ash-can — never shall my whiskers be shaved again!"

Matys was very skeptical concerning the possibilities of my success. He extemporized to me quite masterly the idea that, like Christianity, Socialism shall remain immune to adulteration for at least one century. This argument, however, I do not consider as absolutely conclusive, and it shall not deter me from my resolution. I always had fair luck in gambling. I have well conceived that my new role entailed a temporary renouncement of many of my luxuries, as well as a great deal of comfort — and that includes ninety-nine percent of them. For capitalists possessed of my sense, or that of Raymond Robins, are not common. All this had considerably saddened my mind. To renounce life-long enjoyed privileges is not a simple matter. Only an individual with noble mind and a great power could give them up without a murmur. "So it's come to this," I mused, "that our great country, governed by the people and for the people, shall perish from the world."

"There you are mistaken," commented Matys. "This great commonwealth shall continue to be governed by the people and for the people — but it shall be governed contrary to the advice of your press. The $700,000,000 deficit in your publishing ventures attests to that tendency, does it not?"

"In about a month," said I, "I shall have a respectable crop of whiskers, so let us prepare to return to Chicago by the first of July. From there we may be able better to observe the last kicks of the expiring civilization."

(To be continued.)

Editor's note: In the next issue of *One Big Union* the noble Quasimodo proposes to relate his vicissitudes in Chicago. If the board of directors of his corporation won't have him interned in Kankakee, he may be be able to tell us some absorbing adventures.

The Conscience of a Dum-Dum Bullet
Chapter 2

In Which the Author Ventures to Feel the Pulse of the Proletariat's Temper and Scorches His Hand.

I REALIZED that if I was to become a great leader of the Reds and was to conduct their revolutionary scheme to a successful abortion, I must mingle with them; that I, to gain readily their confidence, in my external appearance, must resemble one of them. All this necessitated a comprehensive preparation. Not only have I ceased to shave, but also to wash and to change my laundry, and I slept with my clothes on. Thus by the first of July, after I practiced proletarian habits for full six weeks, I acquired so wretched an appearance that I resembled the ideal of a Bolshevik even more closely than Nicolai Lenin himself, and I felt that I was in a sufficiently propitious shape to go to Chicago and shake hands with my unwashed "brothers." Everything was prepared for our journey and we entrained for Chicago on July 2nd. We traveled in an ordinary Pullman car with the common people and arrived in Chicago in due time.

Having ceased socially to exist as one of the great lords of industry I could not have resumed residence in my mansion on Sheridan Road; hence, I assumed a funny Russian name (which I cannot disclose here) and established myself in a regular hobo bunkhouse in North Clark Street. In addition to securing these quarters, I had Matys rent his in his own name a respectable apartment nearby in which to conduct my business affairs, and to which I had Matys transport secretly all my mail, such as required my personal attention.

During three weeks I associated with all sorts of rebelliously-inclined working men, attended several of their meetings, but was unable to get a definite conception of their political aspirations. However, at the decline of the month of July, as I was perambulating up Clark Street and meditating upon my future glory as the political Moses of the proletariat, and at the same time the saviour of my own patrician caste, my attention became attracted to a soap box orator and a group of men assembled around him at the miniature park in front of Newberry Library. The man must have been preaching for a long time already because he showed symptoms of exhaustion. I only caught a few of his words about capital and labor having nothing in common. Then he announced that Miss Leshetitzky was released from the Federal penitentiary several days ago, that she was in Chicago and was scheduled that night to address this audience. "I am tired," he admitted. "I prolonged my speech only to hold the crowd here until she arrives; her time is past due, and it seems that something is delaying her, so if there is a speaker in the audience he is welcome to the soap box until she arrives." In a flash I got an inspiration that this was an opportunity to make my debut as a Bolshevik orator, and I threw up my hand involuntarily and exclaimed that I would like to take the rostrum for a few minutes.

My offer was accepted, but when I mounted the box I realized that I really did not know what to say. I was facing a serious embarrassment when I recollected the concluding words of the professional orator, so I annexed them as a nucleus for my speech. "Comrades and fellow citizens," I cried, "I come from Minnesota. I am a hunter and a trapper. The former speaker was right when he said that we have nothing in common with capital. Strabo and Aristophanes have said the very same thing, only in Grecian language. I won't repeat the exact words because you would not understand them. And when St. Paul commanded the slaves to obey their masters he did not mean to say that their interests were common. He simply was solicitous about the skin of the slaves, anxious to keep it from the harsh contact of the master's whip. If we obey our masters we simply do so to keep out of jail." I noticed signs of impatience in the crowd, so I thought I had better become more radical. "It is like this," I continued. "When I am attending to my profession in the woods my interest is conflicting with that of the foxes and minks and the beavers — my interest is to get their skins and theirs is to keep them, don't you see?" The audience exploded into a tremendous applause and shrieks of *bravo*. When the applause subsided, I resumed my speech. "There is a similar discrepancy between yours and your bosses' interest. You ought to be careful how to vote. If I was to be elected to an important public office I would honestly look after the interest of the working man. I would boost your wages; I would fight for your personal liberties, see to it that beer and schnapps is restored to you, so that you could resume your pursuit of happiness. I thank you for your kind attention." I stepped off the box. There was only a feeble applause for the second part of my speech, which I deemed the best and most important.

A big, black Negro mounted the box immediately after I stepped off. "I want to say a few words to the trapper from Minnesota," he cried, unceremoniously emphasizing his words with both of his fists. "As long as working men will continue to repose their hope of redemption from the hell of wage slavery into the fickle and treacherous hands of the politicians they shall remain wage slaves. Parliamentarism is obsolete. The proletariat has recently discovered a better remedy for its political and economic emancipation. We, the Industrial Workers of the World, are already applying this new paregoric to all our social abrasions — and I will say to you, brother trapper, that it is as effective as a dum-dum bullet. So magically effective are our politics that the 'captains of industry,' who always were after our skin, are trembling with mortal apprehension about their own. Before the props upon which the profit system rests are completely broken, the most effective way of exacting from our industrial vampires a greater fraction of the fruit of our toil is by keeping a brake upon production. On the other hand, we know that the surest way of inviting our enemies to step upon our neck is by creating over-production. I thank everybody who can understand me and who can read the signs of the times."

His speech was applauded with as spontaneous a fury as the first part of mine. I became dumb-founded to hear such anarchistic utterances, and from a Negro. This must have caused George Washington to turn over in his grave.

When the applause subsided the regular pulpiteer announced the arrival of Miss Leshetitzky and introduced her to the audience.

The woman was about 30 years of age. Her pale, haggard face was rendered prominently characteristic by a pair of lustrous eyes blazing forth penetratingly like the eyes of a wolf. Resting upon me, her sigh eclipsed mine and made me feel strangely uncomfortable, causing my entire body to shiver. I wondered who could this woman be whose mere look causes me to tremble like a goat confronting a tiger. Were I no longer one of the most formidable sharks in the great ocean of this, Uncle Sam's democracy? "Dear fellow workers," the woman serenely addressed the audience. "Were it not for the black plague of capitalism the world would be a happy place in which to live, because the whole of Nature is a work of sublime ingenuity. Likewise the mind of man is tremblant with germs of romance and adventure. Naturally, I would like to talk to you about music, poetry or other noble arts; however, I am constrained to propound the old distasteful subject about the epidemic of profits and its (in recent years) increased virulence. I beg you to be believe me that I can engage in such dissertation only with a supreme repugnance. The foremost point of my mission is to arouse in you abhorrence for work under the present system, because it is upon your toil that the dragon of capitalism is feeding; should you cease pampering it, that is to say, should you stop all production, the monster would die in a short time and you would be permitted to rise to the full dignity of man, to which you were intended by your Creator. All the nefarious acts of capitalism are disguised by some attractive mask. Liquor has not been taken away from you to enhance your morality but to make you more efficient. Cannot we summon enough courage to fling the gauntlet into the insolent face of the apostles of efficiency and profit?

One by one your scant liberties and the traits of your manhood and dignity are being fed up to the moloch of profit. You can no longer make pretense to social superiority over domestic animals. To make hog or cattle husbandry a profitable business necessitates the unsexing of most of the male members of their breed. A similar efficiency scheme is now being experimented with upon man. I understand that some states have already adopted it, and are even now rendering your brothers into eunuchs. Your masters respect neither human nor Divine laws. They would not hesitate for a moment to extirpate your brains if their profits could thereby be benefited. In fact, hundreds of your brothers have already had their brains clubbed out of their head because they dared to interfere with their masters' profits." The woman paused for breath and immediately a deafening applause and savage shrieks exploded in the audience. I never witnessed such a spectacle before. The whole scene revealed to me the immense scope of human passion. I realized that when the temper of the mob becomes as grouchy as that, only machine guns can quiet it.

The soul of the entire proletariat was so completely possessed with the evil spirit of revolt that I also realized that my ambition of becoming their political pope was a fallacy. Only a fool would attempt to pat a mad dog. I elbowed my way out from among the frenzied mob and went to my bunk house.

When I reached the hotel office I telephoned to Matys and ordered him to bring me a decent suit of clothes from my wardrobe at my mansion, and to have my chauffeur appear with one of my closed cars at the eastern entrance of Medinah Temple. (The reader can make a fair guess at my reasons for not having ordered the car to appear at the entrance to my "hotel".) The two hours which were requisite for the proper execution of my orders given to Matys I spent at a nearby barber shop. So when Matys came with my clothes he found my personal appearance again resembling a human being. Thus terminated my ambitious Bolshevist career.

(To be continued)

> In the next chapter of the great von Belvedere's autobiography will be disclosed the amazing secret of how his prodigious intellect was enlisted to combat the impending revolt of the steel slaves, and how he advised Judge Albert Garcia to have constructed in advance and stored in readiness a portable wooden Bastille with a capacity for 10,000 agitators.

The Conscience of a Dum-Dum Bullet
Chapter 3

In Which the Setting in Order of Mexico is Prudently Postponed; and in Which the Author Grants Unlimited Opportunity to General Wood to Grow to the Full Size of Presidential Timber.

IT would be needless to apprise intelligent readers that I had a Turkish bath and a general massage upon my arrival at home; and that the resting in soft bed was beneficial to my lately much-abused body. I am recounting here only such happenings as are of historical importance.

The morning following my resumption of residence at my home, I came across a letter from Judge Garcia, which was sent to me under special delivery privileges and which was lying already two weeks upon my desk. I found the text of this unique communication not only philosophically important, but so flattering to my vanity that I decided to present here its full text:

> Illustrious Sir:
> A great strike is *impedifini*, not only in our mill, but in the entire steel industry throughout the country. I know that you have only some $50,000,000.00 invested in steel, and that were merely the shrinkage of dividends from that source involved your cause for worry would be negligible. However, as the case is shaping itself, the most sacred principles of our free institution are at stake. Collective bargaining, after the recently revised tactics of the workers, is a criminal disguise for collective robbery. If we allow them to organize their "One Big Union" all bargaining will end right there; Bill Haywood, Debs, Simms and Foster shall then send us out the doors while they shall be deciding how to dispose of our property. Sovietism and confiscation would supersede Christianity and democracy. The UBERMENSCH element of our society would be degraded to the unholy level of the working class — and civilization would be no more.
>
> We have the Mexican problem on our hand, a problem in which you are deeply interested. But we cannot tackle it with any certainty of success without having the steel production pushed at least a whole year ahead

of consumption. This we hoped to achieved by the six months' truce between capital and labor which we recently offered to the American Federation of Labor through our government. Due to Bolshevist agitation, this truce was denied us. Scorning the offer of the government is a crime! It must not go unpunished. Production must be enforced. We must see to it that every wheel of the government's machinery be set in motion to save the republic.

You may be surprised, sir, at the familiar manner with which I am approaching you. Now, I do not pretend to be intimate with you, but I am often associating with your closest friends, who imparted to me some of their intimate knowledge concerning your phenomenal patriotism and your almost incredible influence upon the government. A few days ago I had a conference with Morgan and Schwab and in the course of our discussion your name came up and I soon learned that you are the mightiest intellect in the country. I learned that you wrote eleven of Wilson's university famed fourteen points, which eleven points are the only sensible ones and which were virtually accepted by the Paris peace conference. You and Barney Baruch are also credited with the draft of the League of Nations to enforce peace. And the articles which you wrote were so perfect that even General Smooth could not improve upon them. Above all things, you are credited with inducing the President to get us into the war. With your flaming Ciceronian eloquence you have convinced him that our participation was for the good of democracy and humanity. Thus you averted the loss of billions of dollars of American investments. I also learned about several other excellent deeds of yours. You may blush all you want, but you needn't try to disprove these facts.

Now, while we were deliberating upon the new perils to ordered society, we all came to the conclusion that if we were to enlist your aid, your wonderful mind would surely devise some means to aver the approaching revolution.

Should you condescend to grant me an audience, I would present you several concrete facts connected with the situation, such facts as would convince you that this matter merits your distinguished attention. Your reply shall be awaited with anxiety.

I have the honor of remaining, sir, with boundless admiration for your exemplary patriotism, your wisdom and your prophetic vision,

Albert Garcia.

The text of the letter above made me glad that the Judge was seeing the whole situation in the same light as I did. I conferred with him immediately through the telephone and invited him to come in the afternoon to my La Salle street office.

There was a warm greeting when the Judge arrived at my office, because his classic letter caused me to consider him almost my equal. However, we cut short all ceremonies and settled to business. Subjects such as our individual health, or weather, are of little importance when there is disease in the whole system of society, and when portentous thunder clouds are hovering above the entire privilege system of our class. "You wrote to me, my dear Garcia," I said, introducing the subject, "that the entire civilization is imperiled by the activities of the Reds, and that it could be saved only through my intercession. If I am really possessed of such supernatural powers as are ascribed to me by you and Messrs. Morgan and Schwab, I surely am willing to exploit them to so holy a cause. Hence I am eager to hear your suggestions."

The Judge is an accomplished debater, but he was employing a lot of big words. Hence I am presenting here his most important opinions in a simplified form so that everybody could understand them. He was convinced that a strike was necessary, because the workers could be safely subdued only through hunger. But he deemed it imperative that at least twenty-five percent of normal production be maintained and that the meetings of the strikers be curtailed and all radical orators suppressed so as to keep the temper of the toilers within the bounds of safety. "In this way," he concluded, "we shall not only annihilate the newly organized union, but we shall see the defeated slaves resume work at a considerably reduced wage."

I frankly told the Judge that he did not convince me about my assistance being needed, that his plans were as good as if I had made them myself.

"The difficulties," said the Judge, "lay in the executing of those plans."

"Have you a respectable jail in your town?" I asked.

The Judge smiled. "I think it's respectable," he said. "The bars are made from our steel. But upon what charges can the radicals be incarcerated? Promoting of strikes has of late become a lawful occupation."

"There is more than one road leading to Old Kentucky, my dear Garcia," I replied. "Why not charge them with Bolshevism, seditious utterances, disloyalty, pro-Germanism, syndicalism, I. W. W. -ism and criminal anarchism? I simply would have every suspicious character pinched, and have our legal spider entangle them in the Overman spinach law afterward; the war is not over yet, or is it?"

Garcia's eyes commenced to shine. "Great stuff!" he commended. "The idea would be perfectly feasible if our bull pens could accommodate all the rebels."

This last obstacle irritated my temper. "Life is growing more complex every day," I cried with disgust. "The Romans would simply corral the agitators into their amphitheatre and then turn a few hungry leopards or lions amongst them, and the gate receipts of the spectacle would have filled their coffers with gold, while we have instead to keep Judges, jails, guards, deporting commissions and God knows what. I am beginning to feel a hearty contempt for our civilization."

The Judge sighed painfully. "Then all my plans have gone to pieces," he said, resigned.

"Oh no, nothing went to pieces," I said resolutely. "We are going to build jails. It's cheaper than to surrender our fundamental and time honored rights."

The Judge betrayed signs of misgivings. "If we start to build jails before the emergency arises," he said, "we would evoke the suspicion of the public, and if we wait until the emergency is here, then it shall be too late."

No sooner had the Judge spoken than I had a solution for the problem. I showed him that we can build jails secretly. "I can have my civil engineers design a portable wooden Bastille. I can have the parts made in my own factories here in Chicago without even divulging to the superintendents the purpose for which they are intended. You can have your agents place the order with me in their own names, and for some pretended commercial purpose. They can have it shipped to your town and stored in a handy place. When your jails become overcrowded your agents can offer the Bastille for sale, either to the municipal government or to the War Department. With such material at hand, ten common laborers or soldiers can build accommodations for one hundred Reds every day."

"Great Scott! What an inspiration!" the Judge exclaimed in bewilderment. "Now I feel contented that democracy shall not perish. With an intellectual Hindenburg such as you are for our leader, we shall easily surmount any obstacles that Bolsheviks may set in our path."

"Of course we shall!" I fervently averred. "We have thousands of machine guns in the arsenals at the present. We have the sawed-off shotguns which are serviceable and effective at night as the machine guns are at day. And we have all the secrets of the Huns as to how to make poison gas. We still have a million men under arms, while radical speeches are the only weapon which our helots can employ against us — and we have the means of silencing most of them."

"This reminds me of one more vital question," said the Judge. "When the walkout takes place, the entire steel community must be submitted to martial law. Our success shall largely depend upon the military efficiency of the officer whom we shall choose for conducting the job, but I think I got the right man on the string."

"Who is your man?" I asked.

"General Pershing," the Judge proclaimed proudly.

"General Pershing?" I repeated contemptuously. "Why, sir, we may just as well entrust this task to any old woman."

The Judge's eyes popped out. "This comes like lightning from a clear sky. Do you not consider General Pershing as the greatest soldier we have?" he asked in an astonished voice.

"No," I replied simply. "I consider him to be one of the poorest."

The Judge was thoroughly puzzled. "If this is the case," he said, "then why did you recommend him to President Wilson as the leader of our armies in France — or was I misinformed? Leonard Wood was my choice."

I gracefully divulged to the Judge that Pershing's military shortcomings as well as his tenuous intellect were the very reasons for my choosing him for the overseas service. "The best military talent we need right here at home," I declared, "to fight the kaisers of labor. Leonard Wood did not go to Europe because I wanted to save him, that is to say, to keep him handy for a bigger job as, for instance, the one we have under discussion now."

"Future then had no secrets for you!" stuttered the Judge in amazement.

"No," I modestly admitted. "Not many."

After a brief silence on the part of both of us the Judge broke into a plethoric laughter. So completely did he yield his self-restraint to his sentiments of merriment that he lost his balance and fell off the chair. And this laughing fit reacted upon him twice after I had picked him up from the floor and tried to draw his attention to the business at hand. "We are facing a serious thing," I reminded him, after I had helped him to his feet a third time.

"Yes," he agreed. "The situation confronting us is grave, but when I come to think that in a conference lasting less than fifteen minutes you have succeeded in convincing the President that General Pershing was the greatest military genius upon the American continent, I forget that we are living in a serious world."

I asked the Judge if he had any influence with Fitzpatrick, so as to cause him to call the strike when we get ready for it.

"That's the easiest part," said the Judge, laughing. "I only need to insult him. I know his Sinn Fein temper."

Thus our business was completely settled for the present. I invited the Judge to have dinner with me at the Blackstone Hotel. However, no more important matters were discussed that day except at our parting, when the Judge proposed that we promise some definite reward to General Wood. I authorized him to apprise Leonard Wood in my name that if he keeps the impending strike in our basic industries within the limits of the law, I shall consider him as the most auspicious Presidential timber.

(To be continued)

Editor's note: Kernel Quasimodo declined to confide to us as much as a single word concerning the next turn of his dum-dum history. So we approached Matrys, who is his most confidential servant, and promised to him the post of the President of the Academy of Art in the coming I. W. W. society. And he confided to us that Chapter IV is devoted to the promotion of patriotism.

The Conscience of a Dum-Dum Bullet
Chapter 4

(Editors' note: For the benefit of our new subscribers we make here a comment upon the strange origin of this unique story. The honorable Quasimodo von Belvedere, having done his share in aiding the President in starting and winning the war, thought that democracy was saved. So he retired to his hunting preserves in Northern Minnesota and devoted his genius to exploring the nature of the chipmunks. While he was pondering over the cause of the cramp-like jerk of their tails accompanying every cheerp they utter, one of his servants reported to him the news that civilization was tottering and Bolshevism taking its place. This alarmed him so that he immediately resolved to take heroic steps to save it (because his investment in civilization amounted to some $400,000,000.00 according to our vague guess). In his queer attempts to arrest the die of Sovietism the crazed state of the capitalist's mind is so successfully portrayed that his narrative is worth reading twice. The ideas in each chapter are to a large degree independent of the others, hence a synopsis is unnecessary.)

Wherein Matys' Association with Bad Company is Revealed.

THE days following my conference with Judge Garcia, I summoned two of my civil engineers and laid for them the Bastille scheme. To enable them to work upon plans intelligently, I had to take them into my confidence, presenting to them the facts undisguised. This, however, entailed no risk because they were both ardent patriots. After a brief council the two gentlemen of science found the project to be a very simple one, and they assured me that within three or four weeks there would be produced jail accommodations of sufficient capacity to meet any probable emergency. Perceiving they were able to deal with this matter more expeditiously than I could, I turned over to them the whole project: the design, as well as the placing orders for the product and the supervision of the manufacture.

The engineers having been departed, I granted an audience to Cecilia, a clever German girl, who was in my place to spy on my servants. "Cilia," I addressed the girl, as she entered, "I am very busy today, but I shall listen to you if you can tell your story in two minutes."

"I can tell it in less than that," she said, dropping into the rocker. "Do you know that Matys has his best friend in jail, perhaps for life? She could be released on bond, and Matys makes frantic efforts to raise the money."

"Then the person you speak of is a woman?"

"Yes."

"That's interesting. How did you learn all this?"

"The apartment occupied by Matys consists of two rooms and a parlor. Next to his parlor is a room which formerly also belonged to the apartment and communicated with a parlor by the door. This door is now locked and nailed up, but there is a large keyhole through which you can hear without effort any conversation going on in the parlor. Now, I was arranging that vacant room when Okakura brought me a letter from my sister, which came in today's mail. I sat down to read this letter, and the chair upon which I happened to take a seat was right next to the door communicating with the parlor. While I was sitting and silently reading, Matys came to his apartment, accompanied by a man who came to counsel him on a very pressing matter. They both took a seat in the parlor on the other side of the door at which I was sitting while reading my letter. You see I couldn't help but hear them. Had they talked nonsense I should have paid no attention to them, but they talked about money, thousands of dollars. It was this that interested me. The stranger said that the crime of his sister was of the nature such as the capitalistic government never pardons ('That shows that he was the brother of the culprit.') Matys resolved to consult a lawyer immediately. He said that he had three thousand dollars in the bank and pledged that amount as a part of the bond for her release. The stranger presented him and then with an autographed photo of the girl, and also gave him a package of her manuscripts for safe keeping, remarking jokingly that in the house of 'Kernel' Quasimodo the papers were as safe as if locked in the President's vault in the White House ('I suppose the police want that package also.'). Matys accepted the manuscripts with as much reverence as though it was a holy miracle. He declared that the coming generation shall prize the papers as highly as the leaves of grass. This allusion I cannot make out, because it is ridiculous to suppose that grass shall cease to grow so abruptly as to become a rare relic to the next generation.

"When the men left I followed them at a distance through the corridors with the intention of looking out of the window and getting a glimpse at the face of the stranger as he would pass out on the street. But Matys forgot something, and, returning to his room, he almost ran into me. He, of course, had no suspicion where I came from. Therefore he had no suspicion whatever that I know anything concerning his affairs. So he simply told me he was going out, and instructed me to tell your Japanese valet that he went to a dentist. When I took the towels to Matys' apartment afterward, I saw the photograph of the girl, and I cannot imagine why Matys is so crazy about her. A man that has saved three thousand dollars and holds such good position as Matys does can get any number of better-looking girls than she — girls of unblemished reputation."

"You said that the photograph was autographed. What is the name that is inscribed upon it?"

"Feodora Leshetitzky."

"Miss Leshetitzky, Miss Leshetitzky," I said to myself. The name sounded familiar to me. At last I visualized the Newberry Park scene — a frail female figure standing upon a box, her flaming eyes penetrating my entire being like an electric current. I saw myself surrounded by a fanatic crowd, thrilled by her insane utterances and her impassioned eloquence. During these brief aberrations of my mind I also recollected that, while awaiting my turn at the barber shop after I came from the proletarian meetings, that I telephoned to the Department of Justice and had the Leshetitzky woman and the Negro orator apprehended. Little did I suspect then that this action was inimical to the interest of my good friend Matys. I immediately resolved to repair this injury caused to him through my action. But of course I could not act until I heard the story from himself.

I gave Cecilia twenty dollars as a special recompense for her faithful services and advised her to take a broom or a carpet sweeper and go to work for a while in Matys' parlor, telling her I would pass by in a few minutes to have a look at the Leshetitzky photograph.

The girl having departed, I lighted a cigar and went for a walk in the corridors, purposely straying to the wing occupied by the elite of my servants. The door of Matys' apartment was wide open so I walked in. Neither Cillie nor anyone else was there but I had no difficulty in locating the object of my curiosity, which occupied a prominent place upon the writing desk in the parlor.

A striking feature of the photo was the costly attire of the woman. It became her exquisitely, giving her a distinctly aristocratic air. I became still more mystified when I noticed that the photograph comes from the same firm that makes my pictures. The cost of a half-dozen pictures of such highly finished workmanship would amount to some three months wages of a common working girl. The case had all the characteristics of a mystery.

I returned to my library immersed in deep contemplation. There was something strangely attractive about the woman and I felt an irresistible desire to learn who she was. Her attire and her poise in the picture attested not only to an aristocratic breeding, but indicated noble aesthetic traits. I recollected her address delivered to the social scum at the Newberry Park. Anti-American and anarchistic as her utterances were, they attested to a profound culture. It also commenced to dawn upon me that she was a beauty, and my first sentiments of hate for her were now being superseded by sympathy and admiration.

    I needed Matys' opinion upon my recent arrangement with Garcia. Hence it occurred to me that if I invite him for the discussion immediately after his return, while the emotional state of his mind lasts, I may also draw from him a few facts concerning the life of Miss Leshetitzky and his relations to her. I penned to him a note, requesting him to come to my library, and I summoned Okakura to take the note to Matys' apartment.

The Conscience of a Dum-Dum Bullet
Chapter 5

Wherein Matys Predicts that the Government's Exploitation of the Proletariat for the Benefit of the Pluts is Liable to Have Disastrous Consequences to a Free, Democratic Country as to an Autocratic One.

WHEN Matys presented himself before me about an hour later he was very pale and his entire physiognomy betrayed a disturbed mind. After the formal exchange of greetings I inquired solicitously about his teeth.

"Oh, it's a trifling matter," he replied.

"But you look sick."

"Do I? That may be due to worry."

"What is it that worries you?"

"Oh, it is not worth discussing. Everything may turn out well tomorrow. It would be a waste of time to discuss my personal affairs."

"I am anxious to help you. If it is in my power, don't hesitate to tell me what I can do for you."

"It would be blasphemous to surmise that there is anything beyond your power." He said jokingly: "Kindly extend to me a loan of twelve thousand dollars and my troubles shall vanish before the sun sets down."

Although Matys expressed his wish in an apparently light-hearted manner, I knew that he should consider its fulfillment as a tremendous favor. The nature of his request being anticipated by me, I pulled out of the drawer with my banking accessories almost simultaneously with the utterance of his desire. I made out a check for the sum required and handed it to him.

He took the tiny slip of paper with a trembling hand, glanced at it and deposited it in his notebook.

"May I ask of you one more favor?" he said in a timid voice.

"What is it?"

"I would like to devote this afternoon to my own affairs. Two of my friends are in the clutches of the Federal mamelukes of justice. I want to bail them out."

"TWO friends," I exclaimed in surprise.

Matys was silent.

"If that's the case," I continued, "I can have your friends set free in ten minutes if you tell me their names, and we can set forthwith to attend to some of my own business — I am becoming more and more dependent upon your counsel."

Matys hesitated a moment, then he wrote two names upon a tablet. "Political felons," he said, pushing the tablet toward me.

The two names were Feodora Leshiteitzky and Samuel Roberts. I telephoned to my lawyer and gave him these two names with instructions to start an immediate action for their release.

Matys returned my check to me and stammered something in an effort to thank me, but I waved my hand. "No words are necessary," I said. "I know your feelings. I only ask your discretion. You realize, of course, that I cannot afford to become compromised as a patron of an element that's attempting to undermine our government."

"I am deeply moved by your kindness, sir," said Matys warmly. "Some day I hope I may be able to prove to you my appreciation of this great favor."

For the present, I thought, I had been admitted far enough into the confidence of Matys. Hence, I deemed it wise to turn our attention upon a different subject. My uppermost concern was to check the awakening proletariat — to keep it in its place. Should we, the pilots of industry and civilization, succeed under my leadership to suffocate the life-germs of the One Big Union embryo, the whole scheme of the dictatorship of mob would be postponed well-nigh unto the other world.

I asked Matys whether he was sufficiently calm to concentrate his mind upon sociological affairs. Having answered in the affirmative, I read to him Garcia's letter, and I also acquainted him with the most important arrangements between us.

Not only did Matys find my plans feasible, but he admired them and predicted for me a great success — providing my ideas were executed by competent persons. He was truly enthusiastic over the Bastille project, but he warned me not only to have imprisoned more workers than is absolutely essential. "You are planning to establish order in Mexico," he said, "which may prove to be a big task. An undertaking of this nature can be successfully accomplished only by ardent patriots, and prisons are detrimental to patriotism. Men serving terms in your Bastille for no other offense but their struggle for a fairer share of the fruits of their toil shall come out Bolsheviks — conscious of their own temporal interest. Promiscuously populating the Bastilles with discontented slaves would be tantamount to digging the grave for the privileges of your own caste. Prisons are the most prolific hatcheries of revolutionary sentiments. The history of all ruined governments presents to us the facts that the plans for their destruction were made within the walls of their own Bastilles."

"How am I to understand your recommendations? First you tell me how clever my ideas are, and then you attempt to show me that they will serve only to dig my own grave. What then is your actual advice, that the Bastille project be given up?"

"No sir. I agree with you that the strike cannot be won without a capricious Bastille and a skillfully conducted martial state. I also believe that you are the only thinker in the whole United States capable of creating such perfect plans for immediate practical purposes. However, I fear that this method may produce as disastrous *sequelae*, as mercurial treatment inflicts upon the victims of a certain disease. Paralysis, insanity, and untimely death are the well-known *sequelae* of the 'cure.' Is it not manifest that in devising your remedy, you have not given the slightest thought to the after-effects it may cause?"

"You believe, then, that the Bastille cure for strikes which I had devised shall imperil our social institutions with after-effects worse than the disease itself?"

"Exactly."

"What would you propose, then?"

"Nothing. I believe that in the course of general evolution, a change is now due in the economic status of the whole world. I fear that it cannot be arrested."

"Shall we then keep our arms folded while the Russian plague shall be spreading all over the world?"

"Oh, I know well that the privileged caste to which you belong cannot remain inactive whilst this reversion of economic and moral ethics impends. However, it matters little what it does."

"But you have admitted that my plans shall win the strike!"

"Yes, it will be a victory — a cure with after-effects worse than the disease itself."

I realized that Matys' mind was not sufficiently calm to ponder over so deep a subject. He was too preoccupied with the troubles of the two friends. Hence, I dismissed him for the day so he could go and meet them, for they must have been released by this time.

(To be continued)

The Conscience of a Dum-Dum Bullet
Chapter 6

Wherein Matys Voices His Doubt that Seeds of Patriotism Planted in a Musty Sub-Basement Will Ever Germinate.

SINCE the time I discarded my proletarian habit and returned to society I have been approached by several of my colleagues who attempted to interest me in an enterprise of Americanizing the alien and promoting patriotism among the laboring classes. I ignored the subject because I could not see what difference it made to us whether the workingmen understood our Constitution or not. In fact, I believed that we can make them serve our interests better if they remain ignorant of the text of our fundamental state papers, as well as our history. There are very few laws in our Constitution of which I approve. Moreover, George Washington, and especially Abraham Lincoln, made many utterances which I consider utterly un-American. Only a few days ago Mr. Morgan sent me two clippings from the Red press, in both of which the Constitution was profusely quoted. One of the clippings was an article from the *One Big Union Monthly* published by the I. W. W.s in Chicago. And the other was an editorial from the *Liberator*, a magazine published by some Soviet maniacs in New York. Now, if the Constitution is good for them, it is not good for us. Publications controlled by me never quote any of the Red clauses of the Constitution. And as to Abe Lincoln, we celebrate him for the only reason that he is dead. I never worried my head over the patriotism of the masses until after my last discussion with Matys, in which he brought my attention to the fact that the wars which we have occasionally to wage upon other nations, cannot be conducted successfully with an army devoid of patriotic sentiments. He also pointed out the sad circumstance that our industrial conquests, achieved by more or less harsh tactics as they are, tend to weaken, or totally extinguished the patriotism of a large number of men. Considering all of the above circumstances, it comes at once obvious that, inasmuch as in our conflicts with labor some of the loftiest patriotic sentiments have to be stunned, pulled to the ground and trampled down, that patriotism must be artificially fostered to replenish the waste. Serious reflection upon the above facts led me to the conclusion that the brand of patriotism which my colleagues advocated, and which they considered beneficial to us, must have been inspired by the exigencies of business which, in its character, may be as foreign to the patriotism of the founders of our Republic as the Christianity of today compared with the character of

Christ. I was wondering how such puerile thoughts could have originated in my sensible head that my fellow capitalists desired to spread among the rabble the text of the Constitution, or the doctrines of Lincoln, or other hot-heads of the past. I recollected that at the "CHICAGO CLEARING HOUSE" session Mr. Julius Rosenwald introduced me to one of the executives of Rotschield & Co., Mr. Ezekiel Veilchenduft, as one of the apostles of the practical Americanization movement, and that Mr. Veilchenduft invited me to visit his "Loyalty School" held every workday at the sub-basement of their State Street store. I telephoned him and inquired for particulars, and when he repeated his invitation, I consented to visit his show. We set the date for the following morning.

> **THE ONE BIG UNION MONTHLY**
>
> The new I. W. W. magazine, "The One Big Union Monthly," is now off the press and will be ready for distribution in a few days.
> It is 64 pages and contains about 50 articles and 15 cartoons, besides bulletins and reports.
> There never was such a labor publication issued before.
> Every I. W. W. member should subscribe immediately. Locals and other organizations should send in their bundle orders at once.
> $1.50 per year; 15 cents per copy. Bundle orders, 10 cents per copy.
> Orders and remittances should be addressed to "The One Big Union Monthly," 1001 West Madison St., Chicago, Ill.—Adv.

Butte Daily Bulletin (Silver Bow, Montana) February 26, 1919

The idea occurred to me to take Matys with me, because day from day I was becoming more dependent upon his opinions. In case the Loyalty curriculum was defective, I knew that he was capable to discern its weak points, and he would indicate them cheerfully. I summoned him and laid the matter before him.

"What do you think of the scheme?" I asked him.

"Have little faith in it."

"Why?"

"I presume that, if Mr. Veilchenduft's loyalty seed had any value, he would not plant it in a sub-basement."

"That's a premature criticism."

"It's merely a suspicion. However, I am much interested, and I would like to ask Mr. Veilchenduft a question or two upon this modern subject."

"I am offering you the opportunity."

* * *

At ten o'clock the following morning, Matys and myself called upon Mr. Veilchenduft at his office at the store, and I introduced Matys as my friend and a literary man. Mr. Veilchenduft was excessively polite to both of us. He behaved more like a valet than a gentleman. He took us to the elevator and we descended to the basement, where the mechanical service ended. From thence we descended to the sub-basement by a stairway. Before we reached the bottom a musty smell assailed my nostrils, and I was beginning to realize once more that one cannot learn much without incurring discomforts.

The Loyalty meeting was held in the shipping room, and was already in progress when we arrived. The assemblage was just saying the Lord's Prayer. After the Prayer a thin-haired girl with a sickly face sat to the piano, a stern-featured old man seized a fiddle, and the pair set forth to play "My Country" with commendable alacrity. The crowd arose and sang the hymn, their voices were permeated with so much fervor and conviction as if the country really belonged to them. I looked at Matys, but he seemed to pay no attention to the singing. He was studying a wall which was decorated with two Old Glories and the pictures of President Wilson, Abraham Lincoln, J. J. Pershing, Foch and Kitchener of Khartoum. Veilchenduft was singing. His behavior harmonized with the crowd so perfectly as to make you think that he was in his own element. After the hymn, the impresario of the Loyalty show called upon Mr. Gans to deliver a speech. Mr. Gans was a handsome Jew about forty years of age. He related the history of his own life, how he was born and raised in dire indigence somewhere in Russia. How he emigrated to England and reached Liverpool penniless. His life was a continuous tragedy until some ten years ago, when his fate drifted it into the merciful hands of Rotschield & Co. With Rotschield & Co. he found a steady job. By and by he fell in love and got married. He started at nine dollars a week and by now had worked himself up to a position that pays twenty dollars. Having thus arrived at the climax of his story, he bowed to the audience and retired to his seat upon one of the benches.

A short fat Negro was summoned next, to give a piano solo. He rattled off a lively Fox Trot, and gave the "Sweet Home" for an encore. The applause he received showed me that the crowd had a great appreciation of music.

Following the Negro, Mr. Neuman, the head of the shipping department, made a speech. He appealed for a general co-operation and increased production, urged the employees to be on time, and scored the dishonorable practice of one employee punching the card for another who happens to be late. His speech was very sensible.

The "Star Spangled Banner" followed — and finally the oath of Loyalty was taken. I will give here the form of the pledge because I think that every child should know it:

> I pledge allegiance to my flag and the Republic for which it stands. One nation indivisible with liberty and justice for all.

I also found a beautiful prayer in the hymn-book that was handed to me by the impresario, *viz*: "O almighty God, Continue Thy gracious protection to those who have gone from among us to battle for the freedom of mankind... " etc. This prayer is of no use now, but it shall come handy again in our future wars.

A Prayer for our Boys Over There

O, Almighty God, continue thy gracious protection to those who have gone from among us to battle for the freedom of mankind. Behold them with favor, help them with the grace of courage, give them victory; and keep us worthy of their sacrifice. Amen.— *Henry Barrett Chamberlin, Vice-President Rotary Club of Chicago.*

"All this is very nice," I said to Vielchenduft, "but this foul air is suffocating me. Let's get out of here."

Mr. Vielchenduft proposed that we go to his office, to which Matys and myself agreed. However, Matys desired to make a closer acquaintance with Mr. Gans, so he would not go with us immediately but promised to join us later. Mr. Gans was coming our way which made us linger for a while. As he was passing us, Matys approached him courteously, shook hands with him and congratulated him upon his fine speech as we moved to go.

I thought well of the Loyalty training but I did not care to give Mr. Vielchenduft my opinion until I had consulted Matys. So when we arrived at his office, I engaged him in a discussion upon the League of Nations. Mr. Vielchenduft's opinions upon the subject were very crude. He soon admitted that international affairs were beyond the limits of his intellect, that he left their adjustment to greater minds. Nevertheless, he professed an explicit faith in the covenant. "The President had at his command the advice of the foremost financiers of the country," he said. "I am satisfied that they saw to it that the covenant embodied substantial benefits for American business."

At this juncture Matys came in, and in his presence I thought it safe to touch upon the Loyalty propaganda. "What do you think of the whole affair?" I asked him as he took a seat.

"Like all things human, the system is imperfect."

"I appreciate criticism more than flattery," said Mr. Vielchenduft. "What fault do you find with it?"

"The President is appealing to every patriot to increase production, and here you withdraw the workers from industry for nearly an hour every day and have them sing — and what a singing it is! Their lungs must be full of mushrooms."

"Oh, the production does not suffer by this," said Vielchenduft. "We make them work an extra hour in the evening."

"Oh, that's different," said Matys. "But would it not be more patriotic to turn your slaves out into the street for these forty or fifty minutes and give them a chance to breathe some fresh air?"

Mr. Vielchenduft looked upon Matys thoroughly puzzled. "My dear sir," he said, "that's Bolshevism, what you are preaching. If you give the slaves too much taste of fresh air they would want to remain in fresh air all the time. This would ruin our business."

The discussion was becoming tedious and I was becoming hungry, so we left Mr. Vielchenduft, and Matys and myself went to the Congress Hotel to lunch. During the course of the meal I asked Matys what kept him at the sub-basement for half an hour after Vielchenduft and myself left him.

"I wanted to see more of the inferno, and particularly the place where Mr. Gans performed his important task. His department consists of a room about thirty feet long and fifteen feet wide. It adjoins a lavatory. A counter runs through the whole room, behind which there are two white men and four Negro wenches packing crockery and chinaware. The stench there is much more offensive than at the shipping room because there the merchandise is being packed in manure. Of course, officially the material is called straw. However, its filthy appearance and its nasty smell readily convey to my imagination the idea that several generations of pigs had been bred and nursed in that straw before the farmer decided to part with it for the price offered by Rotschield & Co."

"The conditions cannot be quite as bad as you present them. Mr. Vielchenduft may be capable of neglecting the interests of his employees but he is too clever to drive away his customers by sending them merchandise packed in unclean material."

"There you are mistaken. These Jews are catering to the most indigent element. 'Bargain' is Mr. Vielchenduft's motto. Give 'em a bargain and they'll come back. If you want to convince yourself I will buy there a couple of cheap plates, have them delivered, and then I will open the package in your presence."

"No, thank you. I would not want the delivery wagon of Rotschield's to stop in front of my house."

"I did not finish my story. The manure is surrounding the packers and there is always several inches of the compost under their feet."

"Who is to blame for that? Suppose you were one of the packers. What would prevent you from shoveling the manure aside and keep it from under your feet?"

"There is no room to shovel it away. The handyman whose business is to supply the packers with the compost brings the stuff in basket-fulls and dumps it over the counter until it reaches up to their necks."

"When the crew goes home, do you think the straw is left upon the floor until the following day?"

"Of course it is. This is against the rules of the Fire Department, but rich firms do not have to obey the law. The whole place is infested with roaches, which breed in the accumulated filth. Hog cotes are being cleaned once in a while but Rotschield's packing rooms are never cleaned. To work men under such health-killing conditions, and at the same time preaching to them patriotism, is the limit of moral corruption."

"You did not tell me yet what Mr. Gans is doing there."

"Mr Gans is a checker. He brings in the baskets with the merchandise, re-counts the items, and places them on the counter. His task is arduous. It's perhaps his consciousness of the confidence which the firm reposes in him that renders his work easy. However, I detect a flaw in his character. He may yet become a Red."

(To be continued.)

The next installment will deal with the physician's report about Woodrow Wilson's Brain being loose, and how Herr von Belvedere prevented the report from circulating among the public.

The Conscience of a Dum-Dum Bullet
Chapter 7

How the Doctors Looked into President's Wilson's Head While Secretary Tumulty Was Asleep; and the Appalling Disorder They Beheld There.

WHILE the philosophical discussion between Matys and myself was peacefully proceeding at the Congress Hotel dining room, our attention became attracted by a great tumult in the street. Several newsboys were shrieking at the top of their damaged voices: "PRESIDENT WILSON — " ... something awful about the President, but I could understand nothing beyond the name. The horrible idea occurred to me that he might have accepted the amendment to the X article of the League of Nations; or that Senator Lodge, or perhaps Hiram Johnson, threw a bomb at him. I sent out Matys to find exactly what the commotion was about. Matys was almost breathless with excitement as he returned a few minutes later with a newspaper in hand. "*The President is insane,*" he stammered, and he laid before me the paper containing the following headline in a four-inch type:

PRESIDENT'S ILLNESS SERIOUS
LESION OF THE BRAIN, DOCTORS SAY

Never in my life did I get in such a rage as this piece of news provoked in me. "What incredible idiots these doctors and editors are," I said to Matys after I somewhat calmed. "Of course, the President's brain is loose, and always was so. I knew that when he was Presidential candidate for the first time. That was the very reason why I reversed my policy and contributed to the Democratic campaign twice as much as I did to the Republican. At the bankers' conference in New York when we then arrived unanimously at the opinion that Wilson's mind was weaker and much more plastic than that of T. R. But what's the object of letting the cat out of the bag at this time?"

Matys gazed at me in astonishment. "Do you really mean to say that you supported Wilson in his Presidential aspirations, despite your knowledge of the cracked condition of his brain? How did you expect him to carry on the business of the country?"

"We never expected the President to conduct the affairs of the country. We do this ourselves. Did we not have Barney Baruch, Julius Rosenwald, Schwab and Redfield helping him? Even in Paris we had our men, pushing our interests to the front. The President devoted most of his time to gambling. He played solitaire for fabulous sums, and (according to his panegyrical biographer) kept an accurate record of his gains and losses. He never kept accurate records of anything else. And yet he became a great President. In popularity he reached a point never attained by a mental weakling before. This attests to the omnipotence of our press."

"Your political machinery is still in good order," said Matys. "You still have the power to elect the President, as well as any other official. I freely concede that you can take any half-wit from an asylum for the feeble-minded and make of him a popular statesman. The process is simple. After you have your man selected you place him in the hands of a skillful politician to teach him several absolutely meaningless phrases. Next, you hire a circus man, who will give him lessons in gesticulations — train him like a monkey. Then you spend a couple of million dollars in having him exhibited throughout the whole country, and have him to demonstrate his dignified motions, and repeat his phrases like a parrot. Then, if you place a sufficient number of your agents at the polls, well supplied with one dollar bills and '*visum repertums*' for Scotch whisky, your victory shall be an easy one. Because the American people are intelligent, you know. But what are you going to do with victory? The worker will present to you his claims, irrational more than ever, and he will use his *industrial* power to enforce them. You can fool them no more. Governmental cabinets have of late become groups of mere puppets. The seat of omnipotence is now in the process of transition from capitalism and its political fakirs into the hands of labor. The One Big Union idea is the one big menace to your rule, and you haven't done anything as yet to check its phenomenal growth. There is a big job still ahead of you."

Maybe the warning Matys was giving me was good, but I had no time to analyze it or act upon it. My mind was preoccupied with the administration scandal that was being so thoughtlessly advertised in the press. I realized that if we are to retain the business advantages and benefits derived from President Wilson's administration, the news concerning the interior of his head must be promptly suppressed. Hence, I dismissed Matys from my company, went to the hotel lobby and dispatched a code message to a lawyer who represented my interests in the city of New York. I instructed him to see immediately Mr. William Randolph Bristlebane and offer him a sum up to two hundred thousand dollars as a recompense for keeping the reports concerning the President's mental state out of his press.

The following morning I went to New York in person. There I called into conference seven of the leading financiers. When I explained the harmful possibilities of exhibiting the mental shortcomings of our Chief Executive, they all agreed to make a liberal contribution to the cause. Thus the day was saved.

The Conscience of a Dum-Dum Bullet
Chapter 8

How the Coal Diggers Spoiled My Winter's Vacation.

THE steel slaves, who were on strike for several weeks already, have been almost subdued. Judge Garcia and General Wood assure me that they have the situation well under control, that my Bastille was doing effective service and our victory was already in sight. So I intended to go for a couple of months to Palm Beach for a rest. No sooner did I give my orders to Okakura to pack my trunks for the contemplated vacation, than the coal miners came out with fantastic demands and threw down their tools. The situation appeared very dark, because the fuel supply at hand was hardly sufficient for a month. Fortunately the law was on our side. President Wilson and Mr. Palmer soon discovered that the war was not over yet. Strike was an act of treason, giving aid and comfort to the Kaiser at his wood-pile. That was an admirable idea, sufficient in itself to prove that at least two percent of the cells in the President's brain were still alive. While the government's machinery was set in motion on behalf of our cause (to suppress a criminal strike), a funny incident happened which is worth noting here. Mr. McAdoo made a squeal about my two-thousand percent profit during the war. Of course it is a trifle more than he made on the New York tunnel. It is even more than the government realized on the railroads under his management. But there are no limits to profits a shrewd businessman can make. Obviously, Mr. McAdoo wants to run for President on the Red ticket while Debs is serving his penitentiary term.

Well, we soon succeeded in having the strike called off, but the production of coal was not resumed and the situation was assuming an alarming aspect. I was becoming nervous because the officials at Washington would not guarantee that the government would succeed in breaking the strike, illegal though it was. The officials of the A. F. of L., while sympathizing with us as usual, shared the consternation of the government and admitted that they lost control of the rank and file of the coal diggers, that they could not get them back to work without offering them substantial inducements. I was willing to grant them a twenty percent increase, providing the government would allow us to raise the coal about forty percent. To this Dr. Garfield objected. Of course, the government would not break its time-honored custom of allowing us anything we wanted, but he feared that the Reds might interpret this as an attempt at profiteering and cause new complications.

Therefore, with the popularity of the Fourteen Points in our mind, we decided to set the wage increase at fourteen percent and postpone for a few weeks the doubling of the price of coal. It was also understood that the President would make generous promises to the men. Promises of the President will make a good impression, and they will not be binding upon us. Under this arrangement, Dr. Garfield thought he could easily induce the strikers to resume work.

Although the outlook for resuming the operation of the mines was fair, the demonstration of the coal diggers' power alarmed me. I could not help but realize that our power was slipping away from us. Of what use shall it be to us to control the government, or dictate laws favorable to our interests, if the working class form the habit of disregarding orders of the authorities, defy the laws and ridicule injunctions? Because, should the miners resume work (as is expected), the credit will be due to the cunning and chicanery of the President rather than to their respect for the law. The proper thing for the businessman and the government to do now is to keep the workers from becoming conscious of their strength.

Before a week elapsed it became apparent that Dr. Garfield's proposal, and, especially, the President's generous promises, were sending the miners back to work. I was anxious to know what Matys thought of the situation now, because when the strike broke out he predicted that the miners would win. I summoned him to the library, where we usually held our discussions upon sociological and economic problems.

I was reading the *Chicago Daily News* when Matys came in. "Are you following the movements of the strike?" I asked him, as he accommodated himself in the chair on the opposite side of the table.

"Not now any more, the strike is lost."

"Lost for whom?"

"The miners, of course," he replied with disgust. "These fools return to work with no more tangible an inducement before them than the word of the President, now, when they needed to wait only three or four days more and they would get everything they wanted: six-hour day, five-day week, and they could dictate almost any wages they pleased."

"But the settlement we are offering them is fair."

Matys said nothing, but laughed. So I read him the two ensuing paragraphs of an editorial in the *Daily News*:

> Chicago now faces a grave condition instead of a mere probability. The coal shortage is acute. Drastic measures of conservation have had to be adopted. More are to follow. Railroad service has been curtailed; so-called non-essential industries — which are essential to those who earn their living in those industries — are deprived of coal. The business day has been reduced to six and a half hours.

It is to be made still shorter next week. The daily loss to labor and to those who conduct business enterprises is tremendous.

Where does the responsibility for all this rest? At the present time it rests with the leaders of the organized miners. The national cabinet and the fuel administration fumbled the issue at first, but the final proposal made by Dr. Garfield and approved on its merits by the entire cabinet was eminently fair, reasonable and sound. It offered the miners full justice, if not immediately, certainly in the near future. It granted them an increase in wages to cover the exact ascertained increase in the cost of living. It provided for a commission to study and remove all other grievances and maladjustments in the industry.

"You are right," he said. "The whole administration agrees with you and Dr. Garfield that your proposal is eminently fair and sound, that it offered the miners full justice, if not immediately, certainly in the near future, and offered them an increase in wages to cover the exact ascertained increase in the cost of living. It provided for a commission (this is very important) to study and remove all other grievances, etc., etc., etc.

"The government offers full justice, but not immediately. Of course not — there is no hurry with justice — but why is it, sir, that if the government takes a notion to do injustice or violence to something or somebody (as, for instance, the I. W. W.s), why is it, sir that the brutality is committed immediately?

"Why is it that you offer the slaves an increase in wages to cover the exact ascertained increase in their cost of living? Suppose the eighty thousand toilers who are slaving for you in your coal mines, your steel mills, your steamships and a score of other fields should organize into one big union and appoint a commission to ascertain the exact amount of profits you need, to pay for your three meals a day, the upkeep of your wardrobe, etc., with an occasional dime for movies, and an occasional two bits for castor oil or epsom salts — "

"That's enough!" I cried, interrupting him. "You are an anarchist! It's talk like that that's undermining the discipline of labor and destroying the fabric of the government!"

Matys apologized. He admitted that he made an irrational digression from the subject. He also admitted that the offer the government was extending to the miners was generous beyond all precedents. "But," he concluded, "what would you do about it should the miners reject Mr. Garfield's correct figures? You are not dealing with justice. It's power you are confronting. Should you become accosted by a lion in the jungle, you would not stop to argue about justice. More likely you would climb the nearest tree. Superior power recognizes no laws or injunctions of a lesser power. The American proletariat is a lion which is as yet unconscious of its power. But Nicolai Lenin, the archangel of the wage slave, is sounding his mighty trumpet day and night. Well, sir, I predict that before a year elapses, the American slave will be wide awake — then we shall have a new interpretation of justice, a new code of morality and a new aspect upon the purpose of life."

"The only conclusion I can draw from your talk is that you favor Bolshevism. Your radical proclivities are a puzzle to me, because you are above the proletariat. You wear clean clothes, you work less than six hours per day and less than five days in the week, and perhaps you have a substantial bank account to your credit. Why should you wish to wreck a system which is benevolent to you?"

"Surely, this is an absurd guess you are venturing at my conviction. The fact is that I would do everything in my power to save capitalism if I thought that it could still be saved, because I believe that with your patronage I have the chance to become the President of the United States. Or shall you yourself take the job? I would become to you what Kernel House is to President Wilson. I would become the American Rasputin. Unfortunately, the doom of capitalism is sealed. Capital and labor are clinched in a mortal struggle. In my capacity as a philosopher, I foresee the proletariat emerging from the conflict victorious, but there exists not affinity between my prescience and my political sentiments. You may wish your friend to recover and at the same time realize that his case is hopeless. On the other hand, you may wish your rich uncle to die and dream about the adventure you would have with the money that he would leave you, even if all circumstances indicate that his lease upon temporal sojourn has a better standing than yours."

"Do you really believe that the One Big Union dragon shall have its teeth fully developed within a year?"

"Yes sir, the next Summer shall be the hottest in the history of our Republic."

I was getting an acute headache, so I dismissed Matys and summoned my physician.

(The end of the First Part)

EDITOR'S NOTE - von Belvedere is at present on a yachting excursion in the Southern waters. As soon as his nerves recuperate from the strain of his strike worries he will commence to write the second and the most romantic part of his story.

Quasimodo von Belvedere, Max Bodenheim, unknown, Emma Goldman.

Your Next President

by Trevor Blake

ALAS! The second and most romantic part of *The Conscious of a Dum-Dum Bullet* was never published, and may have never been written. But fear not, for Quasimodo von Belvedere writes again as your next President.

In the following essays, von Belvedere devotes himself to the common good. He comments on current events, runs for President, write plays for the edification as well as the entertainment of his audience, and... for his troubles? Is hounded by the authorities unto a frustrated silence.

Your obedient servant, this editor, first learned of Quasimodo von Belvedere through his nomination speech and endorsement by the Industrial Workers of the World. von Belvedere mentions the "Deestrick of Lake Michigan" in his nomination speech. This is a quiet tip of the hat to another Chicago-area eccentric, George "Cap" Streeter (1837 – 1921). Streeter claimed a patch of land on Lake Michigan that was made up of rubble, garbage, silt and (his own) shipwrecked steamboat, declaring it the District of Lake Michigan. As the President of this micronation, Streeter announced he was exempt from the laws of Chicago, Illinois and the United States itself. He was a thorn in the side of the City of Tomorrow until his demise; Chicago, in turn, honored him by both founding the Streeterville neighborhood and erecting a statue on the corner of McClurg Court and Grand Avenue. How much more must be the glory flung upon the broad shoulders and about the radiant head of Quasimodo von Belvedere! Let his visage adorn the nation's currency, let school children learn his words by rote.

Jazz-Age Chicago made Quasimodo von Belvedere the Independent Superman he was. Being the the more or less complete story of his life and work, it is necessary to consider the man he was before and after Jazz-Age Chicago. His secret identity, as it were.

The man who became Quasimodo von Belvedere was born in Bohemia. Bohemia was a kingdom located in what is now the Czech Republic. His name was, probably, Walenty Noga. As with nearly every detail of the mustachioed imp behind von Belvedere, it is difficult to be certain this is our man. There is a "Walenty Noga" in the book *Książka jubileuszowa Dziennika Poznań 1859-1909*[1]. Is it he? Don't ask me. It is also not entirely clear which of the death certificates in his name apply to his person, nor in which of several graves his remains may reside.

---

[1] Poznań: Czcionkami druk. Dziennika Poznańskiego, 1909.

During Prohibition Quasimodo von Belvedere operated a speakeasy called "The House of Corrections" in the Gold Coast district of Chicago. This bar had interior design on the theme of a prison. Our hero was in part identified by a particular distinguishing feature revealed in the pages ahead.

Hon. Quasimodo von Belvedere is Criticizing the Government

ONE of our clever correspondents obtained from von Belvedere two important political statements which we present here in full.

The President deems that the adopting of the Knox Peace Resolution would be an ineffaceable stain upon the gallantry and honor of the United States. He goes on, saying: "Have we sacrificed the lives of more than 100,000 Americans and ruined the lives of thousands of others and brought thousands of American families an unhappiness that can never end, for purposes which we do not now care to state or take further steps to attain?"

To a sane business man this statement appears ridiculous. All that was attainable from the war we have already attained; we got more than our share of Germany's trade, and we do not want any cash indemnity; in that respect our national honor is very scrupulous, you know.

Furthermore, Germany is not reduced to a naked skeleton; why should we waste any more of our time upon her? I count the President among my most devoted friends, and it would be unkind on my part to make any further derogatory comments upon this curious epistle of his. God knows that there is not a single individual within the borders of our fair country who has a better knowledge about the true reasons for which we went to war than the President himself.

Our correspondent then asked Mr. von Belvedere if he did not think that the natural resources of Mexico were too precious an asset to be left in the hands of such barbarians as the Mexicans are. Quasimodo gave him an admiring look and commended him upon this truly American mode of reasoning. "That is my motto," he said. "Make peace with Germany and then devote all of our spare time to disciplining Mexico and establish an American protectorate over her."

After this, conversation was switched to the Presdiential race, and our correspondent quoted the ensuing aphorism from Mr. Gary's after dinner hallucination: "The next President of the United States must be able, wise and well-informed; of unquestioned honesty, morally and intellectually; eminently fair and impartial; frank and sincere; broadminded, deeply sympathetic, courageous, sturdy and well-balanced (this is not a slam at Woodrow Wilson); and above everything else, loyal to the Constitution and the law of the land."

Quasimodo laughed at this. "Such a President," he said, "would have been all right a decade ago. If these thirteen points of my friend Gary's were a sufficient qualification now — then we should elect him, or Mr. McAdoo. These are the only two honest souls I know. However, I see trouble ahead; such a situation as we are confronting can successfully be coped with only by a good soldier."

"I see," said our scribe. "You are going to vote for General Wood."

"Not only that," says Quasimodo, "but I shall have two hundred thousand of my dollars vote for him also."

Quasimodo von Belvedere, Whose Ambition It Is to Quit Working, And to Become Your Next President

Editorial excerpt: "... we came to remember that I. W. W. tradition speaks of '[abstaining from endorsing any] political parties' but says nothing of independent candidates [so we] hasten to endorse the independent Presidential candidacy of Quasimodo von Belvedere, whose nomination speech will be found in this issue."

Nomination Speech Delivered Before National Convention of the Intellectual Elite of America, Assembled at the House of Blazes, in Chicago on September 16th, 1920 by QUASIMODO von BELVEDERE - Candidate for the Presidency of U. S. of America and the Deestrick of Lake Michigan. Running on the more or less Progressive Ticket of the Independent Superman Element.[1]

LADIES and Gentlemen:

The lady obstetrician, who was summoned to officiate upon the occasion of my advent into this world, could not swim — hence she could not cross the creek which intersected the path leading to our hut; the bridge having been carried away by the flood. When the time was overdue and no other means were employed to facilitate my birth than lamenting and praying I lost patience and I elbowed my own way towards the light. The above history is faithfully recorded in the family Bible. Now, if Mr. Cox or Mr. Harding had arrived into this world unassisted by the goose-lard-mongers, would they not have told about it in their nominating speeches? Of the three of us, there is no doubt, I am the fittest to play poker in the White House. However, the nomination cannot be imposed upon me unless I am given a running mate of my own choosing. I demand that William Gibbs McAdoo be nominated for Vice-President; Herbert Hotstuff Hoover is my second choice, but McAdoo is a much better worker — he would save me the costs of keeping a janitor, a butler and a few other expensive servitors.

The honors which are to be bestowed upon me this evening have been vaguely foretold thirty-five years ago. When I was three days

---

[1] There are two printed versions of this text, differing only in a single sentence.

old, a small circus was passing our village and encamped at a nearby caravansary. Among its curiosities was a blind gypsy girl phrenologist, who could estimate the intellectual caliber of any human creature by passing her fingers over his pate. Hearing about these miraculous traits of this prodigy of a gypsy, my father hurried to the circus tent and fetched her to my cradle. "This is the brat," he said to her. "If you can tell me that he is good for any thing, I will pay you a dollar." The girl groped my head all over and found there wonderful bumps. She readily ascertained that I was destined for brave intellectual exploits. As she accepted the dollar from my father and was turning to go she murmured to herself: "If this child lives long enough to use his head for mischievous purposes, some people will be glad and some will be sorry." This prophecy shall come true tomorrow. Surely, Mr. McAdoo shall become wild with joy when he will read our chairman's telegram, conveying to him these glad tidings that I choose him as my running mate — on the other hand—upon their perusing of my speech in the morning papers — Cox and Harding and even Christensen shall become sorry that I ever was born.

Comrade Debs is a serious rival. Were he turned loose, the country would witness a mighty contest. I am afraid of him. Fortunately, he still has to serve more than eight years for the crime the Government committed upon him, so he can make no speeches. I am in favor of his being set free — but not until after the election.

General Wood was an intrepid candidate; he was my choice; my bet of $5 was placed upon him. The odds were eight to five; so certain I was of his victory in the Coliseum that I made plans in advance to place the whole stake of $13 upon McAdoo. The nomination of Harding prevented me from collecting it and my finances became demoralized. I needed fresh air, so I went on North Clark Street for a promenade. As I passed the Radical Book Shop and was about to turn to Trotzky Square, I was accosted by a beautiful girl. "How do you do," she whispered aloud, at the same time bestowing upon me a tantalizing smile; and the look she gave me was violently eloquent. I gallantly offered her my arm, and, as we proceeded toward Chicago Avenue, the direction for which she appeared to be bent, I recounted to her the sad story how I had risked my last $5 bill upon General Wood, and how Harding had robbed him of the nomination; and how there were still two days until my pay day. The girl jerked her arm loose from mine and contemptuously pushed me away from her. Women are constituted upon so practical a plane that they are capable of sympathizing only with the man who wins; and this is the reason why I joined in the Presidential race and why I would promise the people almost anything in order to win. Personal grievances toward Gov. Cox I had none. I did not bet on the success of Mr. McAdoo.

I could not bring myself to believe that the attainment of justice was possible in the Democratic Convention any more than in the Republican. These two old parties are so foul with corruption that a good man has no chance in their camps. I hope that Mr. McAdoo will fare better in the House of Blazes. He trusted in our fair play so explicitly that he did not deem it necessary to attend our convention and personally guard his interests. His absence shows that he is becoming modest. My own presence in this convention is not due as much to the lack of modesty as to the inchoate consciousness of my political importance, which impelled me to come.

More than a year ago a hungry dog strayed to Mr. Harding's front porch. Mr. Harding came out of the house with a sandwich and offered it to the dog, and THE DOG DID NOT TAKE IT. Dogs are more cautious than men. They no longer trust the candidates of the old parties. Many virtues have been hurled upon my rivals since their nomination. Assiduously as they are learning to wear these new moral appendages, they feel in them uncomfortable and unnatural. "They are family men" is being trumpeted by the kept press. Perhaps they are. What of it? The assertion that they do love their wives is also ridiculously extraneous. If they did not love them someone else would. Women may be capable of preserving vacuum in their heads, but not in their hearts. Many a mediocre husband with his vitality already waned, still desperately strives to pander to the ravenous erotic appetite of his wife with no other motive than the unchristian and egotistic wish to keep her from becoming enamoured in some musician, a poet or any other poor devil of an artist, who, although performing the noblest mission in the world, are too poor to afford to keep a wife of their own. Artists are instilling harmony into life and arraying even its most homely features in rhyme and rhythm of superlative grace. Of all men, artists are the most worth of a woman's love; they are instilling into life the soul of harmony and beauty-arraying even its most homely features in rhyme and rhythm of superlative grace[1].

No family man professing the sublime love principles of Jesus Christ would boast of his monopolizing a source of temporal blessing which he himself is no longer capable of enjoying, and for the want of which the souls of his fellowmen are perishing. Considering all these circumstances seriously, I am for absolute and unconditional practical morality such as was advocated in the indignant ululations of Jezabuku, Shoumonshua and Harlipook. All the illicit pagan traffic which is so efficiently exposed by the aforementioned Shoumonshua; and who, for lack of a better word, terms it Kumiar-jaka-kuti, is being carried on to this very day — boys

---

[1] This final sentence is found in one printed version of this essay and not the other. — The Editor.

and girls meet in the dark for this unauthorized purpose. Neither Mr. Harding nor Mr. Cox do propose to put a stop to these things, where as I am toiling for the past five years already upon a scientific book in which I strive to prove by the very words of the Scripture, that a generous lady never counts the kisses she bestows upon her lover — and that a fat bone will always precipitate a fierce conflict among hungry dogs.

The Non-Partisan-Social-Democratic plank in my platform reads as follows: "I am for public ownership of all the debts that my generous Administration may incur." To capture the votes of the I. W. W.'s and the Communists I shall yet amend this plank so cleverly as to give my definite, and unconditional pledge that the red stripes shall not be expunged from our national emblem during my administration — if I can prevent it.

To offer a practical inducement to Big Business I planed out the ensuing little two by four plank: I stand for single taxation and double gross misrepresentation of the good American people.

The women of the whole country are being solidly lined up in my cause. It was a curious incident through which I won their support: A friend told me that in Lincoln Park there was being held in captivity a baboon whose blessed buttock was resplendent with all the gorgeous colors of the perihelion of a rainbow. "That's the kind of a baboon I want to see." I said to myself, and forthwith I went to have a look at this strange animal. When I arrived at the spot, the baboon was exhibiting his hind part to a middle aged, pale-faced lady. She was contemplating this pulchritudinous symphony of colors with profound interest. As I joined her in admiring this eighth wonder of the world she slyly backed out to a corner, where she gave her face a calisthenic treatment with a puff which was sprayed with red powder on one side and purple on the other. When she reappeared at my side at the rail I looked upon her and noticed that she had succeeded in embellishing her faded physiognomy with imitations of two of the colors exhibited by the baboon, and she appeared to be happier and more hopeful than she was before. Obviously, she was endeavoring to excite my aesthetic senses. I appreciated the adversity which her matrimonial ambition must have been encountering in this present commercialized society. My sympathy was readily aroused and I resolved right there to say to her a kind word of encouragement. Having introduced myself as the Uebermensch party's candidate for an independent President of the United States, I declared that every woman was entitled to a husband, according to my Christian and humane platform; that she will get one when I become elected; and that she won't have to make her face as beautiful as that either, I said, pointing with earnest emphasis to the vari-colored back of the ape.

This straightforward declaration of fundamental democratic principles produced a deep effect upon this honest woman. With tears in her eyes she thanked me for my righteous attitude toward her oppressed sex. Forthwith she slid her hand into her stocking and produced therefrom a two dollar bill and contributed it to my campaign fund. She confided to me that she had considerable influence over Miss Alice Paul and that she hoped to enlist her in my cause to tour the country in my behalf. But it was this two dollars which enabled me to stay at home one day and compose this great nomination speech — every word of which was deliberately intended to inflict a merciless lash upon the knavish back of the plutocratic henchmen who want to fool the people, and who don't know how. Scoundrels and hypocrites! Only yesterday they considered me to be harmless, but tomorrow they will behold my righteous wrath portentously hovering over their nefarious domineering ambitions. Like a Gibraltar, a philosopher equipped with so sublime a gift of pre-science as I am, shall always be towering high above the seas of a charlatanic herd. The most their mad waves can accomplish is to splash my feet. The new order we are approaching is a reign of ochlocracy. Like infuriated meteorological elements, massed for a catastrophic play, the awakening power of the enslaved strata of society shall prove irresistible. These new forces will not suffer to be directed by a "family man" or any other cheap receptacle of conventional respectability. To render the soul of the masses articulate, Providence has fashioned a special criterion: of political sapience. Does not every pulse of your blood make you conscious of this fact that I am the new prophet whom God sent to this world in His last desperate effort to save civilization? Let Hon. A. Mitchell Palmer lay his iniquitous hand upon this prophet and the earth shall be shaken in its foundation; and the sun shall become dark.

I challenge the Senate Investigating Committee to examine my campaign finances and prove that my fund to date exceeds the sum of two dollars, which I voluntarily admitted. My rivals of the two corrupt old parties are said to have a campaign fund of $14,000,000, and they have not as yet made a better speech than any inmate of any of our Asylums for Feeble Minded would, if he were brought under the influence of a quart of 60 per cent virulent moonshine concoction — While I produced a masterpiece of epochal oratorical importance. Such noble logomachical achievement can be attained only with such campaign fund as comes from above. Should I become victorious in this Presidential race — will not this be a positive proof that God is with me?

I favor the immediate settlement of all financial obligations of Europe towards the United States. Our debtors cannot pay in Cash, BUT THEY HAVE IN THEIR CELLARS GOOD STUFF TO DRINK! Hence, upon my assumption of the executive power, my first official act shall be to dispatch the entire American Navy to the shores of Europe, and to collect from our debtors $12,000,000,000 worth of champagne, cognac, beer, brandy, whiskey and gin, and perhaps, some of the old, seasoned German schnapps. When the Navy brings the cargo to our ports by the Act of Congress, the cheaper brands of the liquors shall be distributed among the people, while the noble ambrosial liquids shall be reserved for the servants of the people. By a Presidential proclamation a month shall then be set apart for the purpose of drinking these liquors, and for celebrating our regained liberties.

Any Leagues of Nations to enforce peace should have been created before the war commenced. To organize a League of Nations to enforce peace after the forces of destruction had spent themselves, is as idiotic an effort, and its success as impossible, as that of attempting to have one's house insured after it had burned down. Batiushka Woodrow Wilson was in office more than a year while the war was being prepared. He witnessed the setting in motion of the massacring machine, and he did not throw into its gear as much as a single one of his fourteen points. Never before had the American people had so genuine an occasion to be ashamed of their Government as they have today.

RECONSIDERING THE 14 POINTS.
The One Big Union Monthly. Volume 2 Number 7 p. 29

Tradition of the country requires that the President be a married man. You need not worry about that. There is a peach of a girl in my neighborhood upon whom I keep a hungry eye. I shall continue shining around her, and, if you nominate me, I may easily win her for my wife. The only objection she advances against me now is that I am lazy — that I am not earning enough to support her. This objection will vanish when I become elected President of the United States. A clever President can easily earn one million dollars a year — no matter how lazy he might be. Now, this girl is possessed of many charms; I would not attempt to enumerate or describe them on this occasion, because Beauty has no place in politics — nevertheless, I can assure you that she has more influence over me than the church. All men are threadbare creatures, enduring a despairing existence until they receive the blessed sacrament of life which is administered to them in the form of the first kiss from a loving girl. Likewise, a woman deprived of the influence of a loving man feels most wretched, and she is most happy when in his impassioned embrace. So noble a creature is my girl that my soul is craving much more violently for her than for the Presidency, or for the salary and the contraband back-sheesh that's connected with the office. Should this exalted maiden consent to become the First Lady of the land, I shall become the happiest of all Presidents that ever existed. Caressing her and writing lyrics upon her lofty traits shall become the sole concern of my life. This sacred mission shall keep me continually so preoccupied that I shall never find time to introduce any new reforms, or to devise new encroachments upon your liberties. The legislative branch of the government shall be busy drinking the cognac and the champagne for several years to come. Hence, I can honestly assure the people of the United States that, during my occupancy of the White House, they shall be as free and as happy as if they had no President at all.

I thank you for your intelligent attention.

Campaign Speech

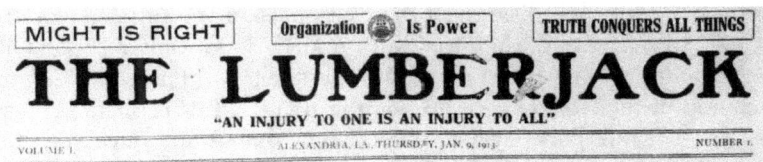

"MIGHT IS RIGHT" according to the Industrial Workers of the World in their newspaper *The Lumberjack* Vol. 1 No. 1 (January 9, 1913) p. 1.

The Nomination Speech is published and sold by
VINCENC NOGA
245 W. North Ave., Chicago
Watch for von Belvedere's great novel
THE CONSCIENCE OF A DUM-DUM BULLET
it will soon be published in book form.

Delivered before a miscellaneous crowd, surrounding his racing car.

FELLOW Gentlemen, Comrades, Workers, and Lady Voters:

One of the immutable biological laws is THE RULE OF THE STRONG. Human society is so constructed that weaklings can rule sometimes; but only by the means of a machinery of power, built by their strong predecessors and bequeathed upon them.

Today, the monster engine of our government is being operated by weaklings, wholly incapable of giving it intelligent care. It is only a matter of time (a very short time, indeed) when this colossal engine will fall apart in hopeless ruin. Again the short-sighted historians will say *that the revolution came all of a sudden*. Fortunately, I am here before you today to give you the true history of the impending social re-adjustment. A few years ago disagreeable squeaks commenced to issue from the capitalistic power plant which was supplying the current of life-energy to our democratic government. The noise interfered with the sleep of the captains of industry, whom some of you prefer to designate by a less respectful term. Those captains supplied Mr. Wilson with 14 *pints* of a well known American oil, bidding him to soothe with it all the abrasions in the rickety machine. Being unable to locate the actual points of irration, and being anxious to dispose of the oil, he used his best judgment and poured the oil upon the fly wheel; the fly wheel splashed some of the oil into his face, and with the rest messed up the floor of the whole political edifice, making it slippery and dangerous to walk upon.

To avoid all such disagreeable experiences in the future, Woodrow resolved to relegate all the dirty work upon his assistants. He sent Kid Palmer and Battling Baker to adjust the machine. These two amateur mechanics attended to every lubricating point, treating them profusely with ashes, sand, gun powder, pitch, brimstone, grape juice and goose berry wine, but the squeaks of the machine were steadily increasing, until they developed into deadly groans. The Captain Kidds of industry became alarmed and decided to transfer the *instrumentum regnorum* into strong hands. T. R. being gone, they find General Wood to be the strongest man in the land. They offer him the job, providing he devises a satisfactory plan to fix the domineering machine. — And lo, and behold! the general proves equal to the occasion, he's got a wonderful plan already drafted. His generous friends rent for him the Chicago Auditorium Theatre and arranged for him an opportunity to address the American people in person and tell them all about his plan.

Needless to say that I participated in this memorable event. (The bulls intercepted me at the gate and searched me for bombs and other death-dealing weapons; finding none, they finally let me pass.) Well, I still was able to secure a prominent seat so that I could see the general at a close range; hence my story is authentic. This is what happened.

General Wood arose from the soft and warm lap of Marshall Field III and he addressed me and the rest of the audience as fellows: "Fellow Citizens: I am glad and proud to be with you tonight. The American people are a great people. I am one of them, and I am willing to serve them." (He did not say how he was willing to serve them; because he ran short of breath, he stopped to fill his abnormal chest with the pleasant air, exhaled by the brave financial Field Marshal, who stood behind him. When his lungs became replenished and his jacket stretched like a Bavarian duddlesack he proceeded as follows.) "The troublesome engine of the government is be coming more noisy every day. It's been proven that the Democrats know not how to fix it. Now, I know how to fix it. I will seize a huge sledge hammer and fix it with a single blow." And he swung his mighty arms, by way of illustrating his future official exploits. He was rewarded with a tremendous applause, my applause and that of Marshall Field being the most spontaneous and most enthusiastic.

In justice to the valorous general I must explain here that he employed military language in his address and that, in quoting him, I have not used his exact words — no man ever was correctly quoted by his friends; but words are not as important as ideas, and the radical ideas of General Wood did not appeal to big business, with the exception of Captain Marshall Field.

The Republican Convention chose to nominate a timid man — a puppet with no ideas of his own. It would be ridiculous to speak of him as a leader; and a brave race, such as we Americans are, is not likely to suffer to be pushed about, or to be driven all the time. This singular incident brings our political history to a climax. Never before was such a dire puzzlement offered to the innocent mind of the American voter — a dark horse of suspicious character is being imposed upon him, and he is not allowed to examine his teeth until he buys him.

I hope that the soldiers cannot be fooled in this clumsy manner. Had he a son, says Mr. Harding, he would wish for him nothing better than "a wholesome term in the U. S. Navy." I understand that during the war all relatives of draft ages of President Wilson chose wholesome and safe services in the Navy, while all the brave men joined the Army. I have a great admiration for the returned heroes; they have more voting power than those who did not return, or those who returned in coffins. I am prepared to offer to them a bonus in the form of an elegant edition of my speeches.

After General Wood, I was considered by my friends as the biggest Presidential timber in America. I am a superman, this fact was incontestably established by the spectacular manner in which I was born. Mr. Harding himself declared that he is not a superman, although nobody ever suspected him of being one — his protestation was as superfluous as if I would declare that I am not a jelly bag. Not being a superman, Harding is unfit for a superhuman undertaking.

Both Cox and Harding, my principal two rivals, are well known to the whole nation. If either of them had a reputation behind him, such as would recommend him to the confidence of the people, they would not need all the millions of dollars of campaign funds in order to become elected. Jan Hus and Savonarola accomplished infinitely nobler tasks than to secure a good government job for themselves; or to institute reforms such as are outlined in the platforms of the expiring two old parties; and they had a very meagre campaign fund.

I read in the papers that the Democratic bosses are extorting contributions of half a month's wages from the government employees. I proclaim most indignantly that the candidate, for whose benefit this shameless robbery is being carried on, does not deserve to be elected. The proper place for such a candidate is the rock pile at the Penitentiary of Leavenworth.

The practice of the present operators of the Department of Justice is to protect the rascals and to punish the innocent and the brave. Upon my assumption of the executive duties of the President of U. S. I shall make it a matter of official routine to get my daily physical exercise by whipping all such arrogant scoundrels out of the sacred temples of Justice until the standard of fairness, for which our Republic strove from its very birth, is securely established.

I thank you. Kindly clear the road and let my car pass.

My Nearest Approach to Death

QUASIMODO von BELVEDERE

who caused a political landslide at the last election by withdrawing from the Presidential race at the last moment in favor of Harding.

Some ten years ago a Chicago paper offered an attractive set of prizes for authentic stories upon the theme "My Nearest Approach to Death." I joined into the contest by offering a sketch of the following personal vicissitude. My story was not considered as fit reading matter for respectable people then, but fashion has changed since:

DEAR Editor and ye wise judges of the death contest:
The perusing of your column caused the most frightful reminiscences of my brief life to float to the surface of my mind. I do not remember the exact date, but it occurred during the panic in 1907-8, about a week previous to the famous speech delivered at the Convention Hall in Kansas City, Mo., by Mr. W. H. Taft. I was penniless for the first time in my life. Having arrived in the above said prosperous city at about 3 o'clock in the morning without knowing what to do or where to go, I followed involuntarily a homeless dog. As I was passing through a quiet residence district my attention became attracted by a man with a wagon distributing milk to his customers — going from one rear door to another, conscientiously depositing at each of these doors a bottle or two of his lactal commodity. When hungry, men as well as beasts of prey are most susceptible to inspiration — thus, without conscious effort, my mind begat a glorious idea. I followed this milkman at a reasonable distance, sneaking quietly to these rear doors previously visited by him, and emptying the contents of the bottles he left there into my voracious throat. Having had thusly treated about a half-dozen bottles, my stomach commenced to grumble at the overtaxing of its capacity. But being a skeptical philosopher, I feared that I might not meet with such a piece of good luck for many days and that, if I should have plenty of time to digest it... so I drank another pint and nothing happened, except that my vest stretched like an overturned drum and two of its buttons yielded to the strain when I stooped to put the empty bottle quietly at the threshold. As I left that back porch I blessed myself in the complacent contention that my appetite was appeased for at least a week to come. But, a minute later, I was surprised to find myself at the rear door of the next house — the bottle was there — what's the difference, I thought, one pint more or less — there shall be a lot of time in which to digest it, I foolishly reasoned. I was about to stoop for the bottle when the door sprang open and a young lady attired in a lily-white night robe appeared upon the threshold, appraising me with an unfriendly glare.

"Does here life Mr. Mieczyslaw Popychowies?" I addressed her in burning embarrassment.

"No Greeks in this house," she snarled most impolitely, whereupon she picked up the bottle and slammed the door before my face.

When I reached the sidewalk and wasn't as yet half recovered from the unpleasant surprise, a heavy hand fell upon my shoulder and secured a safe grip upon my collar. Looking my rude assailant into his face, and perceiving that I was in the relentless clutches of the law, the skin and muscles of my body contracted so violently with fright that about a gallon of milk squirted out of me through my mouth, landing with all its explosive force squarely into the face of the policeman whose prisoner I was. He released his grip upon my collar so he could rub his eyes with both his hands — and, by the time he recovered from his uncommon surprise, there was the distance of a city block separating us. And, of the two of us, I was the fastest runner. So, there you are.

Two Pickles, a Rabbi and a Bishop

Vincent Noga, Jack Jones, D. Isaak Miller, and Bishop Fallows

A gallery of foreign born radicals performed the exceptional at the Dill Pickle Club last night and sat in awed silence as Bishop Samuel Fallows, the principal speaker, outlined the history of the United States in an Americanization talk. Gone were the cryptic witticisms and the ribald buffoonery which usually interpolate speeches at the club.

The purpose of the meeting was to protest against anti-Semitic propaganda. The blame for this in the United States was laid at the door of Henry Ford by Jack Jones, head of the Club.

After calling the United States constitution the greatest document of freedom ever written, the Bishop sketched the history of the Jews in America, paid full homage to the race, and warned his hearers to join in a defense of the nation against disturbers in Europe.

The meeting ended with the passing of resolutions condemning Mr. Ford and his associates for "circulating century old misrepresentations regarding the Jewish race" and calling upon members of all races and religions to "join with the Dill Pickle Club in putting an end to acts so un-American."

The History of a Pig and a Sack of Potatoes

Introduction.
Following is the tale of a sack of Irish spuds and an unruly Jersey pig. It is in the form of a three-act play and was sent to a New York magazine for publication. It was returned with the remark that the editor could not understand it. The author Quasimodo von Belvedere thereupon offered him an explanation, printed below. Few men would ever get into jail were they able to invent as clever an alibi as is contained in that letter.

The Rejected Play

Natural History
Act I
Mr. Peterson unloads from his Ford near the hog yard two sacks of seed potatoes, costing him $17.45 exclusive of freight charges, then he runs his Ford into the corn-crib and goes into the house.

Act II
A large, hungry, son of a Jersey duroc champion smells the spuds, breaks through the barb and woven wire entanglements and nonchalantly attacks the costly commodity. All his fellow inmates rush to his aid. Soon the sacks become disemboweled and the spuds disappear as fast as the hogs can pick them. The tumultuous excitement accompanying the feast soon attracts the attention of Mr. Peterson.

Act III
Arriving upon the scene and beholding the tragedy, Mr. Peterson becomes possessed with unutterable fury. Cursing most horribly, he seizes a manure fork and chases the moral derelicts all over the yard.

Curtain

If you like our show, tell it to our boss;
If you don't tell it to your friends.
Nothing in the above protocol is to be construed as criticism of the President, or as opposition to the League of Nations.

The Explanatory Letter

To the Editor of _____

Illustrious Comrade:

Due to the instability of my address the delivery of the rejected pig story was delayed. From tomorrow on, my address will be more or less permanent, as I have just rented a "newly furnished" front room and paid the rent a week in advance. The blissful message that you like my story and have read it more than once sets thrills of rapture racing through my body. Your penciled note in which you accuse me of being obscure impressed me as if explanation was desired. My honest endeavor to comply with this desire may cause me to write to you a longer letter than you may care to read.

Besides being simple, the idea embodied in my story is set forth with impeccable clarity, quite unsusceptible to wrong interpretation by a normal mind. Obviously, you were searching the story for some concealed communistic aphorism, or an anti-Christian parable, which did not exist. Now, I know that the Editors of your magazine won't find in my story things which are not there. But I was not sure about the Department of Justice. It was for this reason that the paragraph was appended to the story in which the author solemnly avers his fealty to the President and his politics. I presume that you endeavored to connect the innocent character of the story with this appended paragraph and gave up the efforts after one hundred days of hard thinking. You were willing to take a chance, but your associates feared that if the story appeared in the _____ its career would end right there. By following the ensuing review of the author's process of thought at the time the story was being written, and during the dozen or so consecutive hours afterwards, the reason for every word appearing in his story will become to you clear as is the reason for every star in our showy national emblem. The Natural History was written in the evening after supper. The author partook of a generous meal consisting of a plate of Boston baked beans, a big roll of corned beef hash, two hot biscuits and four cups of black unsweetened coffee (there was the German mustard on the table, but the author has two witnesses to attest to the fact that he did not touch it.).

While the story was being written, the author attached to it no political significance whatsoever; he then bestowed upon President Wilson or the League of Nations to enforce peace no more thought than did the swine while devouring the valuable potatoes (see article No. II of the Natural History). However, you will recollect, that individuals in whose heads original thoughts germinated were then fiercely persecuted by the government. Hence, after the story was finished and the author went to bed, his mind became gripped by the apprehension lest there should have slipped into his story a word or two which the Department of Justice could possibly construe as disloyal. On a previous occasion the author had been apprehended by Hinton C. Clabaugh's pariahs upon the join recommendation of President Wilson and Henry Cabot Lodge, who charged him with treason, espionage, or something of that sort. The charge was based upon a letter written by the author, the text of which was no more disloyal than the story about the pigs. Haunted by such dire misgivings, the author was rolling in bed and thinking. And the sleep during which the beans and the other viands were to be digested would not come to him. The course his thoughts were taking ran something like this...

Suppose the story was published and an inebriated agent of the Department of Justice would find, or imagine to have found in it, a flaw of some sort. The story would be sent to Washington, D. C. By some vagary of Fate the Secretary of War might be present in Mr. Palmer's office when the story arrived. They would read it together and immediately see therein things whereof the *New Freedom* made no mention at all. From this they would infer that the author does not like the American government. (My shirt was hanging on the back of a chair close to the bed, so I reached for it and wiped off the cold perspiration which was covering my face.) They would lose no time in taking the case before the President. A special cabinet meeting would be called, to which the majority and the minority leaders of both parties would be invited. (Now, my dear colleague, is not my situation commencing to appear a trifle unsafe to you?)

When the cabinet meeting would get in session the President would put it thusly:

"Gentlemen, fellow servants of the people. The people were profoundly disinclined to take part in a European war, but I thought that if we do not participate in the conflict there would be no League of Nations to enforce peace. So I made a brave speech before the Congress and made a few demands in the name of the American people, and the Congress granted to the American people everything I asked for them: war, conscription, Liberty bonds and sedition laws. We have fought for the rights of small nations and have won the universal confidence of the world, and to do the utmost services to humanity and to satisfy the conscience of mankind we must live up to the rules of the sacred Covenant of Nations which was based upon my fourteen points. Now, I do not pretend to have any extensive experience with hogs. My judgment of them may be too severe. Nevertheless, I am certain that they had no right to employ violence in the breaking of the fence. We have sacrificed the lives of 110,000 Americans and ruined the lives of thousands of others and brought upon thousands of American families wretchedness beyond description. We corralled hundreds of Reds into our penitentiaries and have attempted to drive the I. W. W.s underground. If we keep the good work up civilization shall not perish. I am pleased with the services of the Department of Justice in rendering to the nation. At one time I hoped that the Kaiser would be hanged, but there is no law for the Kaiser — he is as hard to deal with as are our profiteers. But thanks to God, the Reds are easy to catch — by the thousands in a single raid. We are so busy catching them that we may never find time to try them before the bar of justice. It may prove expedient to condemn them in bunches like rotten bananas. This is the free-est democracy in the universe. Our heroes have done great deeds and they have not walked like other people, but lo! and behold! they have walked like free men. They were not free to buy beer, to be sure, but they were allowed to buy Coca Cola, chocolate sundae and ice cream, and we do not want to cheapen their heroism by giving them any bonuses, because we would have to impose taxes upon the fair profits of the American businessman; for have we not a free government employment bureau for the returned heroes?

"There is a clear-cut violation of Articles IV, X, XVII and XXVI of the League of Nations to enforce peace in the third act of the story. Mr. Peterson shows a deplorable lack of sound judgement and much illicit haste. In my opinion, the case should have been submitted for arbitration. May I not say at this point that, as a Christian people, it does not become us to resort to pitch-forks to settle our differences. You are here assembled, gentlemen and my fellow guardians of the people's rights, to suggest the most efficient manner for dealing with the problem at hand. If the story of Q. von Belvedere be true, then the hogs he describes must have some red blood in them." (My shirt was already all soaked wet, and still a new crop of icy perspiration was springing up upon my face.) "The hogs had no right to break the fence by violence, if it should be proven that they had been brought to America from Russia, they ought to be deported, every one of them. I would like to hear the opinion of the Secretary of Labor upon this important matter."

Secretary Franklin K. Lane, being rather a furious guardian of the small people's rights, would address the crew as follows:

"Mr. President and fellow gentlemen: Our beloved President is the greatest statesman ever was born from a woman. He's got more brains than all the rest of us put together, and he is right in his exalted opinion that there would be no Bolshevism had the Russian people accepted the batch of principles which he made for their special benefit and which he was magnanimously offering them. I shall always agree with our President, no matter what he says." (Enthusiastic applause.) "Right or wrong, he is our President, and I shall follow his principles as long as I live." (More applause.) "I denounce Judge Anderson of Boston because he knows more about the American Constitution than a patriotic judge ought to know. I also denounce the Socialist Party for having nominated a criminal as a candidate for the highest office of the Republic. The Reds should be deported as soon as they become Reds, and fresh foreigners with innocent minds should be imported to take their places — because there is a lot of work in America which is too hard and too dirty to be performed by the Americans.

"Samuel Gompers and conservative trade unionists are alright. I am willing to act as a chairman upon any commission to settle disputes between capital and labor, and the thirty-one percent suggestion is the only mistake I made. We all make mistakes, except President Wilson. The miners knew it was too much, and therefore they accepted it. I had seven eminent criminologists and two justices of the Supreme Court studying the case, and they could make nothing out of it, so I showed the story to a prominent New York financier and he found the offense much more grievous than it appears on the surface. He found it reeking with seditious matter and pregnant with evil possibilities and his advice was this. 'Our country, right or wrong, my dear Franklin, that's the motto of true Americans. It makes little difference whether the story be true or not — it should never have been told. An individual who would write stories such as this about American hogs is not a good citizen. Take my word for it, Lane, that he is in the pay of the Kaiser. I never have seen a story more pro-German than this. The proper thing for you to do is to have Mitchie apprehend this man Quasimodo and place him into the hands of a patriotic judge.' This advice I think is very sensible, and the proceedings suggested are in perfect accord with the principles of President Wilson."

All of a sudden the author realized that the entire panorama of prospective horrors which were thus crowding the screen of his overheated imagination could still be averted by burning up the story before anybody sees it. He jumped out of bed to execute the cremation upon the manuscript, so fraught with perilous possibilities. He could find no match for a long while, and when he finally found a match and was about to set fire to the story he recollected the warning of Ibsen that it is an awful sin to destroy a beautiful thought. So he inserted the story back into the typewriter and added to it that solemn protestation that the story was not dictated by disloyal sentiments, that nothing contained therein was intended or should be construed as a criticism of the President, or as opposition to the League of Nations to enforce peace. With this explicit declaration of his political convictions, he hoped he could have the story published without putting his life or liberty in jeopardy.

If you will kindly read to your fellow editors the above explanation of all the treacherous circumstances, they may become convinced that the story is less radical than it first appeared to them, and they may consent to giving it space in some obscure corner of your famous publication. If necessary they may print the above explanation with the story, because the American people are prepared to hear the truth, and this explanation would be sure to keep Mr. Burleson from divorcing your magazine from its mailing privileges. The MS. is herewith included. Whether you should succeed in your renewed endeavor of having it published or not, your good will shall be profoundly appreciated. It makes me unhappy that I can do nothing to demonstrate my gratitude to you. Were I living in your city I might contrive to gain access to your shoes and polish them up for you every day, and a brilliant shine I would give them, such as they never had before. In the coming new society I shall vote for you for any sort of a comissar you may run for.

Yours, with admiration, etc.
von Belvedere.

To Whom it May Concern:

This is to certify that every statement contained in the enclosed documents, particularly the one about the author never having touched the German mustard, is as true as an imperfect, and (one way or the other) always prejudiced human being, is capable of making.

QUASIMODO von BELVEDERE

Subscribed and sworn to me this 9th day of August, A. D. 1920

(Seal)

Tula C. Lewold
Notary Public

Asks for Vamp, One Qualifies, Then He...

VINCENT Noga is a member of the Dill Pickle club, whose one-time stable home in Tooker Alley is a magnet for the embryo poets, artists and free-thinkers of Washington Square and the adjacent centers of Chicago's Near North Side Bohemia. While the Dil Pickle is Mr. Noga's avocation, his vocation is officiating as "general director" of the Pizen Pup Kafe, whose six foot facade, nestling between two buildings of large bulk is a beckoning finger to the hungry literati.

Today Mr. Noga took his brush in hand and posted the following notice in the Pizen Pup's windows:

> Female help wanted. Temperamental waitresses with magnetic personality, explosive, artistic, passionate, vampish. Disposition untamed but gentle and loving. Prefer one with inexhaustable account in a dependable bank, a yacht and a racing car. Must have a conspicuous standing in society, a solid character and a unsuspicious past.

Shortly afterwards it was replaced by a second sign reading:

> Proprietor in jail. Be back later.

Miss Florence Cotney, age 19, who called police, said she had only read the first three words of the sign when she applied for the post.

Buffalo Times. January 26th, 1922
Des Moines Tribune. January 24th, 1922
El Paso Herald. January 24th, 1922
Honolulu Advertiser. February 20th, 1922
Houston Post. January 24th, 1922
Nevada State Journal. January 24th, 1922
Spokane Chronicle. January 24th, 1922
Tacoma Daily Ledger. January 25th, 1922

"Pup Kafe No Place for Lady," Says Florence

Bohemia on Trial; Disorderly Conduct is the Charge

It was a great day for the North Side's Greenwich Village in the Chicago Avenue Court.

Bohemia's broad principles of life were on trial. Freedom in personal contracts had been challenged by an intruder who called it disorderly conduct.

At one corner of Judge Lawrence Jacob's desk stood Vincent Noga, "general director" of the "Pizen Pup Kafe," a "hole-in-the-wall" beanery at 818 1/2 North Clark Street. At the other corner stood Florence Cotney of 1244 North LaSalle Street, still smarting from her first excursion into blithesome bohemia.

No Place for Lady

"I am a waitress by profession," she explained, "and I needed a position when I saw the sign in his window. It read that he wanted a waitress 'such as could be found only in Paradise.' I took a chance, and I found out it was no place for a lady."

Judge Jacobs asked Noga how about it. Noga was silent. He waved for assistance and there stepped forward Jack Jones, the tousle-headed President of the late Dill Pickle Club.

"If the court will permit, I shall speak for Mr. Noga," said Jones. The court permitted.

"Mr. Noga," the Dill Pickler continued, "is unable to speak English fluently, although he writes it beautifully. In fact, he produced the most artistic posters the Dill Pickle Club ever had. He is a man of rare intelligence, an artist of rare merit. His collection of phonograph records is unexcelled. He has been offered $200 apiece for some of them."

Granted Jury Trial

"There must be some mistake in Miss Cotney's charge. I'm afraid that she did not on her first contact understand the bohemian spirit. In order that Mr. Noga may have an opportunity to make a proper defense we ask for a jury trial."

Judge Jacobs granted it. Noga grinned appreciation and handed the Judge one of his business cards. It advertised "beef stew, hobo style," and "eat our soup and live 100 years or less. We are not responsible for anything we say or do. Vincent Noga, Culinary Alchemist."

(1924)

House of Correction Patrons May Be Right

Police from the East Chicago Avenue station arrested six persons last night in vice raids made on two "coffee shops." The first place raided called by the owner, Vincenc Noga "The Gold Coast House of Correction," 883 Rush Street. Five men were taken. From there the squad closed in on the Pompeii Inn, 18 East Chicago Avenue, and arrested the proprietor. The police charge that liquor was found in both places.

A Health Recipe

Now that the supreme court allows a sick man to have a pint of whisky every ten days, I would suggest that those dispensers of supreme justice put their wise heads still closer together and brew up another patriotic decision; one that would allow a healthy man to guzzle a full quart of schnapps a day. By the act of such forensic wisdom, Americans would be made the healthiest of all peoples, I am willing to submit this happy scheme to the sober judgment of any habitual scoffer of the dry experiment: would any sensible person be tempted to become sick in order to be allowed a pint of booze every ten days, were he permitted to tipple two pints of it every day, while taking good care of his health?

In addition to placing premium on health, this humane decision would also rejuvenate the patriotic spirit of the people. The disgraceful scenes of wild soapbox orators shouting Down with the 18th appendix! and Down with the supreme injustice! would become a frightfulness of the past.

VINCENC NOGA
Dungeness, Wash.

The Moustache of Quasimodo von Belvedere

Garrets and Stables

The intimate and artistic life of the "village" is passed unnoticed by the rest of the city, to which Towertown stands only for these bizarre garret and stable studios, long hair, eccentric dress, and free love. This is due largely to the fact that certain shrewd individuals were not slow to see possibilities in the commercialization of bohemia. Some of these individuals were of bohemia themselves. A group of young women writers in Towertown organized "Seeing Bohemia" trips, at seventy-five cents a head, and conducted curious persons from the outside world through tearooms and studios bizarrely decorated for the occasion. Tradition has it that the Dill Pickle Club had itself raided two or three times, secured an injunction to make it safe, gazetted itself, and began to charge admission. The Coal Scuttle and the Gold Coast House of Correction were other efforts of Towertown's business men to commercialize bohemia. They were dingy, out-of-the-way places, marked by an ostentatious bohemian poverty-catch-penny devices to lure the slummers who nightly crowd the district. Few real bohemians crossed their thresholds.

The Gold Coast and the Slum by Harvey Warren Zorbaugh.
(Chicago: University of Chicago Press, 1976)

Fine Mustache Betrays Still

Valentine Noga is a bootlegger by profession, but his chief interest and joy in life is a luxuriant moustache, which measures ten inches across and flows like a bannerette when he parades the streets. Friends, who knew of his business, warned him to clip his moustache as he was so easily identified by it, but he retorted that he would sooner part with his life than his beloved hirsute adornment.

He was parading majestically down the streets of Burnham and was observed by William Jones, a prohibition agent.

"Who's the patriarch?" asked Jones of the admiring bystanders.

"That's Valentine Noga, the man with the best alky and the longest moustache in Burnham, or Chicago for that matter," was the boastful response.

"I think I'll measure his whiskers," said Jones as he followed Noga to a building, where Noga tended his moustache and a 100-gallon still. Commissioner Beltler held him in $5000 bond and the still was destroyed.

Salt Lake Tribune (October 19th, 1927)

Long Moustache Proves Undoing of Chicago Man

Wallenty Noga, a diminutive man of 46 years, had one outstanding pride — a ten-inch moustache which he wrapped behind his ears.

It proved his undoing when he was arraigned before a United States commissioner for violation of the prohibition laws.

Mr. Noga pleaded that prohibition agents who said they found liquor at his home had made a mistake in thier identification.

"Do you think we could mistake that?" asked an agent, pointing to Mr. Noga's mustache. The commissioner agreed that it was unlikely and held Noga to the grand jury under $1,500 bond.

His wife was unsympathetic.

"Serves you right," she said. "I told you to shave it off."

Monroe News-Star (October 19th, 1927)

Caught in His Own Whiskers

Valentine Noga bragged that he had the "finest whiskers and best whisky" in Burnham, a suburb of Chicago, prohibition agents charged. He was arrested, being identified by his mustache.

Columbus Daily Telegram (October 24th, 1927)
Dayton Daily News (November 5th, 1927)
El Paso Evening Post (October 28th, 1927)
Pantagraph (October 24th, 1927)
Republic (October 26th, 1927)

Pride Cometh

Among a people that must proceed by stealth to garner its pleasures or suffer the penalties of the law it doesn't do to make one's self conspicious. Wallenty Noga, of Chicago, was fashioned by nature to slip through the net which reformers set to catch the unwary sinner. That is to say, he is a small man who might have been distinguishable in a crowd by no idiosyncrasy of form or feature that he himself could help. But, such is the perversity of human pride, he threw away this protective insignificance in favor of a 10-inch mustache which he wrapped behind his ears. It proved his undoing.

Mr. Noga was arraigned the other day before a United States commissioner for violation of the prohibition law. He pleaded that the enforcement agents who said they had found liquor in his home had made a mistake in identity. "Do you think," asked an agent, pointing to Noga's mustache, "that we could mistake that?" And the defendant was confounded.

He got no sympathy from his wife, who said: "Serves you right. I told you to shave it off." Which shows that, whatever the righteous may think, a mustache like that is a man's greatest enemy at home or abroad.

South Bend Tribune (October 27th, 1927)
The Times (October 31st, 1927)

See also:

Columbus Telegram November 10th, 1927
El Paso Evening Post November 10th, 1927
Pantagraph November 10th, 1927
Republic November 10th, 1927
Lebanon Daily News October 19th, 1924
Owensboro Messenger-Inquirer October 19th, 1924
Sioux City Journal October 19th, 1924

A Frightfulness of the Past

by Trevor Blake

WHAT more, then, can be said by or about Quasimodo von Belvedere, Independent Superman? Have we not sufficiently interrupted his meditations? Let us now draw the curtain and let him return to the silence that was his own before this meddlesome book came to be.

The genius of our hero justifies itself, but mere mortals may prefer to know the sources for this book. All have been assembled and are ready for inspection.

Quasimodo von Belvedere! May he ever discontinue all tonsorial culture of his face! ....*BUT WAIT!*

I was certain that I had finished my book on Quasimodo von Belvedere. I had spent years searching for every jot and tittle of his writing. I had gathered it all, documented it all, put it together in a book, written an introduction, what more could be said? But some imp or intuition whispered no, search just one more time. And how glad I am that I did.

Just one more time I cast out my nets for the Independent Superman of Chicago. And - lo! Only weeks earlier someone had donated an entire scrapbook of photograph, newspaper clippings and letters by and to and about Quasimodo von Belvedere to the Newberry Library in Chicago. It would not have been possible for me to find this scrapbook before, because it had not yet been donated. The whispering imp or intuition guided me well.

I wrote to the Newberry and asked if they could scan the scrapbook for me. To their great credit, they did so and sent me a high-quality reproduction right away. It turned out I wasn't done with my book at all. Some few of the items in the scrapbook I already had in my book, but for the most part the two had no overlap. The size of my book doubled right away.

I felt no compulsion to stop pushing my luck, and so I asked the Newberry if they could pass along my interest in the scrapbook to the person who had donated it. And... they did.

And... she wrote me, on an April Fool's day. So began an ongoing and much-treasured exchange with Chloris Noelke-Olson, the very niece of Quasimodo von Belvedere. Many, many questions I had about our hero were answered, and entire chapters of speculation in my book were quietly excised with none the wiser. While the quantity of my book doubled with the inclusion of the scrapbook, the quality of my book multiplied ten times over from the family stories of Chloris.

Family Stories

by Chloris W. Noelke-Olson

I would be delighted to convey any information you need on the subject of my uncle and his brother, my father. You should be aware, though, that it would be "family stories" from my father's mouth because the only actual face-to-face contact I had with Vincenc was when I was about four years old. I am 84, and probably the sooner we talk, the better.

Vincenc once traveled a lot, but when he moved to Oregon, he became reclusive. He would periodically send small gifts to my older sister and I, but that was the only contact I had with him, except to find a cardboard mailing box in the attic of his house (in Scappoose, OR, which my father inherited from him) containing his ashes and stamped "HUMAN REMAINS." I thought it was a wretched spot to leave a person who was once so gregarious, and tasked my younger brother with the disposing of Vincenc's ashes, and later, our father's and mother's as well.

My brother Daniel Noga, was the one in charge of disposing of Vincenc's ashes. I badgered him (long distance) to do so. Our late mother didn't want anything to do with any of it. Our father, François, and Vincenc had worked in lumber camps and loved the Pacific Northwest.

Neither had any love for religion, though our father and his partner, whom I only knew as "Professor Shemberg" (sp?), used to have good friendships with several priests (especially Father Stoskopf of the Church of the Ascension on LaSalle) and painted the inside of at least one church (St. Clement's on Orchard St.) with renaissance-type stations of the cross and a beautiful tree of life behind the altar. The "stations" were disposed of (sold, junked, stored?) many years back in favor of a more modern style. I have not been in the church since the baptism of my daughter, so have no idea what the replacements look like. I have, though, been assured the golden tree of life still curls and twines.

My brother distributed the ashes of Vincenc and our mother and father somewhere in the forests of Oregon – deep enough in the woods, I hope, for a new development to not endanger them. I loathe developers; they have "developed" so much of the unique architecture of Chicago out of existence, especially when the late Mayor Richard J. Daley was in his long-lasting office.

I am glad that the last time I sifted through those crumbling news articles, I told myself to "find a home for them" and the Newberry Library was kind enough to adopt the lot. Their Curator, Will Hansen, came to the house and I showed him the family photographs and passed them on to him with what little I had been told about them.

Vincenc was a mysterious figure to us children. He sent my older sister Kathleen, a squaw doll wrapped in a blanket and wearing a seed necklace, with a carved face and a body made of sturdy twigs. It was a dignified figure, but Kathleen finally just wanted to clothe it differently and more-or-less destroyed the original clothing while removing it and lost interest when confronted with the rough twig body beneath

He also sent her a ceramic pig bank painted with clover leaves and blossoms. Neither a cartoon pig, nor a realistic one either – just a friendly looking pig, that is now in my possession. Parts of the clover blossoms and leaves wore off in time, but we restored them with nail polish colors. He sent a length of beautifully patterned Japanese silk, which I eventually sewed into a simple dress with "fairy" sleeves. The printed pattern was so beautiful, it needed no embellishment. My daughter eventually took possession of it, and I've no idea what became of it.

That is really all I can tell you about Uncle Vincenc that I know, personally. My late father said that Vincenc's coffee and social enterprise – The Gold Coast House of Correction – was so successful, that the alderman's (or somebody's) son wanted a piece of the action and was trying to convince Vincenc that he needed a "manager." None of the brothers were types one could coerce and when the fellow was refused, the police busted the place and conveniently "found" a liquor bottle under a table. They beat Vincenc and broke his nose – he was a very handsome man up till then – and tossed him into what my mother called "The Hoosegow" (where did that name come from?). Actually, I'm not sure of any of this; I'm just repeating family legends.

I had a photo, which once belonged to Vincenc, of Miss Sidonie Lavallé (who taught jazzy dancing at the Gold Coast House of Correction on certain evenings), a pretty blonde with the short, curly bobbed hair of the era. I have no idea where it has gone, because it was in one of the many photo albums, and now is not there. It is either in the stash I gave to the Newberry Library, or it has moved on in the secretive way of unobserved objects.

My father said Vincenc was much taken down by having his nose smashed and his business trashed and eventually started travelling and became pretty reclusive. I never heard anything from my father about Vincenc being married, and when he died, and my father inherited his house in Scappoose, Oregon, he had been a recluse. My folks and my brother, Daniel, closed their antique and instrument repair business and left Chicago to live in Scappoose. I stayed in Chicago; I was of age, I worked, and had a horse at one of the local riding stables (which have been completely wiped from local memory) and was not moving.

Vincec Noga and Adolph Noga

One of the brothers, Anthony, who remained in Bohemia and had a large family changed names with another brother (it had to have been briefly, I think), Adolph, so he could leave the country without being conscripted as a single man. So Anthony became Adolph, and Adolph became Anthony. I had almost forgotten that. I'd bet the true Adolph, back in Dombrova, probably kept his name, and Adolph, now in Chicago, who was actually Anthony, had to stay Adolph because that's the name he "came over" with. I think Adolph was the first of the brothers to move to Chicago, and seemed to live a conventional life. I had no idea what he did for a living. He was married to a woman whom we all knew as "Babe," a lovely person who, when I met her, was an invalid who finally died of breast cancer after having radical surgery that proved unsuccessful. Adolph died at Augustana Hospital (now defunct), which was located on Lincoln Avenue and Webster Street in Chicago. My father was very grieved at his death.

Adolph, for sure, had no children, nor did Vincenc nor Jozeph, *that my father knew of...* something would've leaked out if he had. Though much goes over their heads, little children have big ears and are putting 2+2 together all the time. Or, I might have been especially naïve and missed a clue, but I doubt that juicy bit of knowledge would've gone over my sister's head. We had no cousins that we knew of, and finding out about cousins would've been immense to us.

A Cheerful Message
to the **poor**
and
Honest
We can teach them
how to **remain**
SO!!!
Private, confidential
one half hour lessons by:

Prof. Vincenc Noga
himself $5.00
and costs
at the
Gold Coast
House of Correction
883 Rush St., Tel. Superior 7934

Instructions in jazzy dancing
by Mme. Sidonie Lavallée

I have no idea when any of them came to the USA except for François, and I do have that information and copies of the relevant documents. It is a given that Adolph and Vincenc preceded François (who left home at age 14). Their mother died, and their father remarried a much younger woman, so she would be a likely source of half-sisters and brothers that we know nothing of.

Our father, after marrying our mother, also lived a fairly conventional life. He worked very hard, and continued painting and playing violin and repairing stringed instruments for the rest of his life. He loved chess and he stopped singing when his children were fairly young, but always practiced his solfeggio on the piano, and sang at home.

He didn't "drink." He'd have a beer with dinner of an occasional hi-ball, but he wasn't a drinker, nor was our mother. He gave up cigarettes after my sister Kathleen was born. They didn't have much money, even though they lived in the "Gold Coast" which is deceptive, because that was also the area where the Japanese from many of the internment camps were dumped – Clark and Division – heavily Japanese.

When my sister and I started school at William B. Ogden (which was on Chestnut Street between State Street and Dearborn – it was later rebuilt on land at State and Oak Streets), I had at least six Japanese children in my class and as friends; and my father was friends with Mister Toguri of Toguri Mercantile (a shop on Clark Street and Locust which moved to Belmont and Clark and is now defunct), who was also the father of the most famous of the "Tokyo Rose's," Iva Toguri, much maligned and unspeakably treated by the USA. She was put in an open cell and her jailers brought groups of people who paid to watch her. Her toilet had no privacy. She was forced to eat and defecate in front of crowds of people. We were ugly, racist people back then, we are ugly racist people now.

My mother wanted our father to teach us Bohemian or Polish, but he said "Nobody speaks Bohemian." And that was that. We did learn some German, but WW2 put paid to that, when anyone who spoke German was suspected of being a spy, especially if foreign.

One side of our block – Dearborn Street for instance – was wealthy homes and apartments, and across the alley on the Clark Street side was taverns, plumbing contractors, drug stores, novelty shops, a theater (the Windsor) and a shooting gallery (legitimate entertainment at that time, not a hangout for junkies, though it probably could have been), and our family's antique store. Societal stratification was more fluid back then.

Vincec Noga in the Gold Coast House of Correction

To get back to the subject of booze, I have no idea if Vincenc "drank." As in being a drunken reveler. He might have been for all I know, but then again, maybe not. My father insisted the bottle that he got cracked for was a plant and the news articles were exaggerations. All the brothers scrambled for work – their jobs cooking on the Eastland, for instance. François worked as a waiter in New York City when he "came over." He cooked and cut hair in the lumber camps where he worked. Liquor was expensive, and Vincenc spent money and put in a lot of sweat equity getting the Gold Coast House of Correction on its feet. People were served in cells, the waiters wore facsimile striped prisoner's jackets, musicians were hired, dance lessons were part of the entertainment, which calls for a band – that argues for money spent, but money spent on substance and not on booze. So I don't really buy him being a tosspot or bootlegger – too dangerous, for one, and the death of his investment of muscle and money. He got cracked in retaliation for refusing to allow a politician's son to take over his clever and popular enterprise, and also got his nose severely broken, probably for making a joke to some cop.

My brother said before he and our mother left Chicago to join our dad in Scappoose after Vincenc died, our father took all of Vincenc's papers and writing and burned everything except some of the ads for the club, which eventually came into my possession. Both of us would have liked to read his writings, but by the time he and our mother arrived, everything had been burned. We'll never know what was there.

Whenever I read about someone in the arts whose papers were burned by a relative, I cringe.

Dan said that our father told him that after the loss of the café, he and Vincenc left Chicago to work in a logging camp in Minnesota, and they bought a used car. The amount of oil that it took to get them on the road and out of the city was all the oil that was in the car, and the engine burned out. He didn't say if they reached the logging camp.

After the three of us children were born, I doubt that our father could afford even a very cheap car. Adolph, who was the prosperous one, owned a small brick cottage on Belmont Avenue, east of Halsted Street, that he and his wife, "Babe," lived in with their little Boston bull terrier, "Bozo." They did not have a car.

For us, buying a car was as unreal a goal as buying a house. We had a store in two locations (serially), where we lived in the back portion and the antiques and instruments were in the front, and François' workshop was in the basement. At 1341 North Clark Street he also shoveled coal into the building's stoker for a break in the rent. During the years when we lived in the Gold Coast neighborhood, we lived in an apartment, and our father had his painting and workspace in the garage of "The Irving" (a beautiful landmark complex that was torn down). The garage was not huge, even though The Irving was huge for the times and shaped roughly like a capital Y with the right arm missing, and had a garden with trees, running through the center of both the buildings from State Street to Oak Street Most middle class people weren't car owners at that time and used the streetcars, L, and subway.

The only automobile that ended up in our family was a 2nd or 3rd hand station wagon that my mother learned to drive after they moved to Scappoose. She was in her 50s. She drove in order to pick up François from the Portland bus stop every day after work. The house they inherited was one story, and not much more than a shack, but François was a talented carpenter and built more rooms, a woodshed, a large work room, and dug out a root cellar for our mother, who canned everything they grew or had excess of. François also made his own wine. He did not learn to drive their car.

Dan also said he has a newspaper article somewhere, about Uncle Joe (Jozeph) who married, and with his wife, owned a bar somewhere in California – possibly San Francisco – because that is where our father told me Joe had been boxing under the name "Billy Hine (sp?), the fighting dishwasher." He said Joe and his wife gave a big boost to a young male singer who later on became a "name," but he doesn't remember whom, and will look to see if he can find the newspaper clipping about the singer.

Did you know anything about both Vincenc and François being hired to cook on the Eastland? Seeing as just about everyone on that boat was a Czech, as were the brothers, it's probable that they were hired as scratch cooks for the pleasure voyage. Our father said they woke up late, but got on the streetcar, figuring the boat hadn't left yet, and were worried, because they needed the jobs and the salary, and as the streetcar was going toward the river, ambulances were passing them in the opposite direction. By the time they arrived at the river, the Eastland had overturned and many were dead – probably some of their friends as well.

François / Franz had no more than a 6th grade education in a village school, but he taught himself an enormous amount and was curious and good at many endeavors. When his mother died, his father married a much younger woman: she didn't like François / Franz, and made him sleep in the barn with the cows. He stole his mother's garnet earrings from her and ran away at age fourteen and traveled across Europe, learning to play and repair stringed instruments in the interim. My daughter, Flora, now wears those earrings. Wealthy people are born with a silver spoon in their mouths – Czechs are said to be born with a violin under their pillow: François and Vincenc played violin, and I carry that tradition on.

I gave the Newberry Library the photo of Jozeph in boxing pose and regalia and also a "photo-machine" 4-photo of Joe's head. He was grinning and laughing – Dad said he had been drinking when those were taken. My brother resembled him strongly when he was younger.

The drawing of Vincenc in a floppy hat with folded arms was done by François. He took the photo that inspired the drawing as well, but refused to think photography was an art form. He studied at the Art Institute of Chicago under Wellington J. Reynolds, and better known classmates were Grant Wood and Aaron Bohrod. François was an American Impressionist and portraitist, and worked in oils, watercolors, pastels, batik, etching, lithographs, Conté crayon and pen and pencil. As far as I know, he never worked in three dimensions.

On the #2 pastiche, the left side view of Vincenc, you can see how deliberately his nasal bone was crushed. He was a handsome man – all the Nogas were – and if he said something "smart" to one of those cops during the bust, they would've made sure his good looks were compromised for all time.

As you see, I still have the "Jesus" photo. I wasn't sure I hadn't given that one to the Newberry Library. It's not in great shape, though. Vincenc, whom my sister, brother and I knew only as a distant and exotic presence because of the intermittent gifts he sent, seemed like a loner. I'm trying to think how likely it might have been for him to be a family man at all, when he was so dashing and his nose was still intact. But the photos "after" show a quiet and introspective man, which doesn't argue for going out and reeling in women to father children upon, but does foster feelings of injustice and the need to speak his piece.

The Maxwell Bodenheim photo I sent is a Photostat I took of the original along with the photo with Emma Goldman, which the Newberry now has. I copied some of the photos while working at an art & advertising studio. I worked in advertising studios for over twenty years on and off, and when the winter indoor polo season started up at the (now defunct) Chicago Armory, I took off to work a string of polo ponies every winter for six years till the Armory was pulled down to make way for the Contemporary Art Museum. I'll never forgive the city for allowing that gorgeous building to be torn down.

The three photos of my dad are thrown in for lagniappe and contrast, the rogue and the classicist. The photo of the angora goats in that group are one of Vincenc's abodes and the goats are his. I think my father said North Dakota, but am not at all sure at this remove of time. When our folks inherited Vincenc's home and they were digging out a root cellar, they came across several goat skeletons.

EXPERT REPAIRING OF VIOLINS, VIOLAS, CELLOS, BASSES
BOW MAKING AND REPRODUCTIONS
52 Years Experience—All Work Guaranteed

Anushka's

The Home of Rare Instruments and Bows

F. R. **NOGA**
Man of International Repute

Phone 227-2765
Postal Bldg., Room 418
510 S. W. Third Avenue
Portland, Oregon 97204

Check out the lower left hand corner of our dad's last business card. These guys didn't half blow their own horns, eh? His studio was in the beautiful old Postal Building in Portland – an atrium building – how I love those few that there are. The Brewster in Chicago on Diversey Parkway is another fine atrium building with glass catwalks and an iron cage lift.

François was getting off the bus near home in Scappoose, and was hit by a car of speeding teenagers without licenses or insurance, and nearly died by the time the ambulance came to take him to the Multnomah Hospital. He spent about six months in traction – everything on his right side was broken, thigh bone punched through his hip, spleen ruptured, etc. That was the end of his business in Portland. He still painted but the concussion affected his sight and his brain. Someone made the kids come to the hospital and apologize – fat lot of good it did him. I think he was eighty-three when he was hit and he lived till age ninety-six.

I must tell you how glad I am to be able to hand these photos and reminisces to someone who can make use of them. When I pick up these molting photo albums, I feel tired, and mostly like throwing the whole lot away. History can sometimes be a burden, and the idea of trying to impart any of this to children younger than my daughter; children who grew up with computers and cell phones, it makes me weary beyond belief. When I was a child, milk was still being delivered in horse-drawn wagons, and that didn't stop till I was about nine years of age. I struggled to learn to add and subtract; we had no machines to do it for us. To convey the world I grew up in to children in the current world is nearly impossible.

I've heard some of those Bughouse Square characters, and have possibly seen some (the King of the Hoboes, Holy Mary?) at Bughouse Square (actually Washington Square Park) though at the time, we louche post-teenagers were out for a lark on a Friday evening and mostly interested in seeing someone "different,' and probably not listening much to what their message was. When spring rolled around, our agreed-upon wisdom was "When the ants are out on the sidewalk, the bugs are out in Bughouse" and we'd jump in someone's car and drive to Bughouse to listen or to heckle. Receiving wisdom was purely accidental, and most of our learning took place in the group of five or so riding stables within a small area of Chicago, and at the Top Hat Lounge and Saddle Club bars. The riding stables supported a variety of social types, from the very wealthy to the very poor and was a rich environment for learning anything you could imagine. Chicago was more fun back then, whatever age you were.

I'm sure Vincenc crossed paths with Stanisław Szukalski, because he was an acquaintance of Francois' and gave him a copy of his first art book, published by Covici McGee. I have that book now, and his second book as well (which contains a small, separate etching on the flyleaf, which I found in a small bookshop run by a friend. My dad said that Stan would walk into the Dil Pickle with a girl on each arm, and wearing a robe and house slippers. I'm pretty sure he meant something like a *djellaba* and *babouches*. So he, for sure, knew Szukalski and no doubt Vincenc did as well.

May 19, 1939

Dear Rolf:

Your permission that I may criticize you was hardly necessary; I am not much of a gentleman and would have given you hell without permission.

The reason I still stick to Roosevelt is because I have no choice. Roosevelt is the only reliable barrier to fascism we have. By concentrating upon our monetary quarrel with Roosevelt now we could possibly defeat the new deal. What would be the result in that case? Would we achieve our monetary reform? Positively not!!! Once the New Deal is pulled down the Hoover, Hearst, Garner black shirts would seize the government, and our heads would go upon the chopping block.

This subject is too big to be treated in a letter.

Your's etc Vincent Noga
Carlsborg
Wash.

over

In the late 1950s and early 1960s, the Gold Coast / Rush Street entrepreneurs were trying for a more sophisticated mien, and called the little setback between the west side of State and Chestnut Streets the "French Village." There was a rectangular raised flower bed sporting an Eiffel tower replica in its center and behind the flowerbed was a bar called "Le Bistro" with a large head shot of "Duke Haslett" who was Chicago's answer to Frank Sinatra and the resident crooner. Tooker Alley, where the Dil Pickle Club was once located, ran along the north wall of Le Bistro, from behind the Eiffel flowerbed west to Dearborn Street. To the north of this setback, on State Street, was Vernon Maury's bookshop – no best sellers – a Beatnik hangout and temple of erudition, and north of that, Slim Brundage's "College of Complexes" (second incarnation, I believe). At that time, I had no idea my uncle had opened the forerunner of this bar and fascinating place of discussion.

Directly across State Street, from the flower bed was our first real coffee house and sidewalk café, "The Roué," which managed to skirt licensing problems for the sidewalk portion because the outdoor portion of the café was still part of the building plat, even though it was not built upon. Old Mayor Daley did not want any sidewalk cafes in Chicago; I've no idea why.

Across Chestnut Street (which stopped briefly at State only to pick up again north of Clark Street) still on the east side, was a more commercial bar / café called "Coq de la Rue." No one I knew went there, it was for tourists. The Roué was where many of the Beats hung out and were served by "Spanish" Mary in jazz pants and a sweatshirt large enough to be off-the-shoulder. She was a dancer and the ideal Beatnik chick, and worked slinging espressos to the hangers-out.

Later on, the house south of the Eiffel flowerbed became "The Front Porch," a venue with many bad paintings on the walls and catering to college jocks and their dates. I was, by then, driving a horse and carriage as a "hip" taxi service, nights, in the Rush Street and downtown nightclub area. I was underage and illegal, but the carriage had a peddler's license.

My late friend, Janet Miller, a red-diaper baby if there ever was one, was also a Wobbly and always helped with the up-dating of *The Little Red Songbook*. She was a great enthusiast of folk music and sacred harp, and though she didn't play an instrument she was an enthusiastic observer and singer. I wish I had photographs of these people and places, but no one I knew carried a camera around with them. Life was very rich back then, even if we had no photos to prove it.

Vincec Noga and François Noga

Maxwell Bodenheim and Vincec Noga

Life is indeed a marvel: I am reasonably sure I'll be cremated by my survivors, but if I had a grave, I'd like a plain stone with my name & dates and "It's Been Wonderful" incised on it. It has not *all* been wonderful, and there will be problems yet to come but I like to be appreciative of what I've had. Thank god I'm not one of those people who have never left their block. I wish I'd have had money and sense to travel when I was young, or get a really good musical education instead of being the seat-of-the-pants musician I am now, but I will do what I can till they put a tag on my toe.

Quasimodo von Belvedere, Independent Superman

Sources

"A clever satire..." *Appeal to Reason* (Girard KS) August 26th 1911 page 3.

Belvedere, Quasimodo Von.: *Quasimodo von Belvedere, Whose Ambition it is to Quit Working, And to Become Your Next President.* Chicago: Vincenc Noga, 1920.

Finnberg, V.: "Reconsidering the 14 Points." *One Big Union Monthly, The.* Volume 2 Number 7 (July 1920) page 29.

"Genius, Interrupted in Work, Throws Water on Landlady." *Chicago Tribune*, September 24, 1913.

Noga, Vincec: "Health Recipe, A." *Seattle Union Record* (Seattle, Washington) (15 January 1927) p. 8.

[Noga, Vincec] von Belvedere, Quasimodo: "Conscience of a Dum-Dum Bullet, The Chapter 1." *One Big Union Monthly, The.* Chicago: General Executive Board of the Industrial Workers of the World. John Sandgren (editor). Volume 1 Number 10, Whole Number 10 (December 1919). Pages 47-48.

[Noga, Vincec] von Belvedere, Quasimodo: "Conscience of a Dum-Dum Bullet, The Chapter 2." *One Big Union Monthly, The.* Chicago: General Executive Board of the Industrial Workers of the World. John Sandgren (editor). Volume 2 Number 1, Whole Number 11 (January 1920). Pages 49-50.

[Noga, Vincec] von Belvedere, Quasimodo: "Conscience of a Dum-Dum Bullet, The Chapter 3." *One Big Union Monthly, The.* Chicago: General Executive Board of the Industrial Workers of the World. John Sandgren (editor). Volume 2 Number 2, Whole Number 12 (February 1920). Pages 51-53.

[Noga, Vincec] von Belvedere, Quasimodo: "Conscience of a Dum-Dum Bullet, The Chapter 4" and "Chapter 5." *One Big Union Monthly, The.* Chicago: General Executive Board of the Industrial Workers of the World. John Sandgren (editor). Volume 2 Number 4, Whole Number 14 (April 1920). Pages 49-51. Chapters 4 and 5 printed together.

[Noga, Vincec] von Belvedere, Quasimodo: "Conscience of a Dum-Dum Bullet, The Chapter 6" and "Chapter 7" and "Chapter 8." *One Big Union Monthly, The.* Chicago: General Executive Board of the Industrial Workers of the World. John Sandgren (editor). Volume 2 Number 6, Whole Number 16 (June 1920). Pages 40-44. Chapters 6, 7 and 8 printed together.

[Noga, Vincec] von Belvedere, Quasimodo: "History of a Pig and a Sack of Potatoes, The." *One Big Union Monthly, The.* Chicago: General Executive Board of the Industrial Workers of the World. John

Sandgren (editor). Volume 3 Number 12, Whole Number 23 (January 1921). Pages 49-51.

[Noga, Vincec] von Belvedere, Quasimodo: "Hon. Quasimodo von Belvedere is Criticizing the Government." *One Big Union Monthly, The*. Chicago: General Executive Board of the Industrial Workers of the World. John Sandgren (editor). Volume 2 Number 7, Whole Number 17 (July 1920). Pages 59-60.

[Noga, Vincec] von Belvedere, Quasimodo: "Is the I. W. W. Going Into Politics?" *One Big Union Monthly, The*. Chicago: General Executive Board of the Industrial Workers of the World. John Sandgren (editor). Volume 2 Number 10, Whole Number 20 (October 1920). Pages 59-60.

[Noga, Vincec] von Belvedere, Quasimodo: "My Nearest Approach to Death" *One Big Union Monthly, The*. Chicago: General Executive Board of the Industrial Workers of the World. John Sandgren (editor). Volume 2 Number 12, Whole Number 22 (December 1920). Page 48.

Noga, Vincec: "European War as the Most Vital Factor..." *The Day Book*. Chicago. September 26th, 1914. Page 24.

Noga, Vincec: "To Avert Future Wars." *Day Book, The*. Chicago. September 4th, 1914. Page 12.

Noga, Vincec: "Why the Doom of Predatory Civilization Cannot Be Averted." *One Big Union Monthly, The*. Chicago: General Executive Board of the Industrial Workers of the World. John Sandgren (editor). Volume 1 Number 8, Whole Number 8 (October 1919). Page 27.

"NOGA (Vincene)* Chicago, Ill. Volcano of Genius; or, The Progressive Lobster." *Catalog of Copyright Entires: Pamphlets, Leaflets...* Books, Group II, No. 8., 1911 page 723

"The Progressive Lobster" *Coming Nation*, February 10th, 1912.

"Two Pickles, a Rabbi and a Bishop." Chicago Daily Tribune (December 13 1920) p. 5.

mogtus-sanlux

publisher

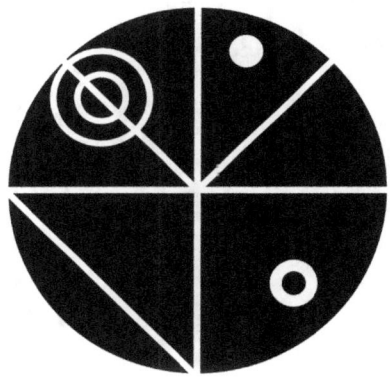

"A procession of the damned. By the damned, I mean the excluded. We shall have a procession of data that Science has excluded. Battalions of the accursed, captained by pallid data that I have exhumed, will march. You'll read them — or they'll march. Some of them livid and some of them fiery and some of them rotten."

Charles Fort
The Book of the Damned

mogtus-sanlux.one
~mogtus-sanlux

MORE BOOKS ABOUT DIL PICKLERS, WOBBLIES, HERETICS AND HOBOHEMIANS

Battle Hymns of Toil & Quivara .... Covington Hall
Beggars of Life .... Jim Tully
Behold!!! the Protong .... Stanislav Szukalski
Black Blossoms at the End of the World .... Selvatico & Pickens
A Child of the Century .... Ben Hecht
Der Geist: Journal of Egoism 1845-1945 .... Blake and Slaughter
The Gospel According to Malfew Seklew .... Malfew Seklew
The Lost Tune .... Stanislav Szukalski
Ladies of the Mob .... Ernest Booth and Christopher Mealie
The Lives and Extraordinary Adventures of Fifteen Tramp Writers . Cutler
The Lost Tune .... Stanislav Szukalski
Might is Right: The Authoritative Edition .... Ragnar Redbeard
Might is Right: The Rebel Poetry of Covington Hall Kevin I. Slaughter (ed.)
Poems for the People .... Carl Sandburg
The Radical Bookshop of Chicago .... Kevin I. Slaughter
The Rise & Fall of the Dil Pickle Club .... Franklin Rosemont
Rival Caesars .... Ragnar Redbeard
A Tramp's Philosophy .... Bart Kennedy
With Claw and Fang: A Fact Story in a Chicago Setting ..Bernie Babcock
Writings & Romantic Entanglements of J. William Schweitzer Slaughter (ed)
You Can't Win .... Jack Black

AVAILABLE NOW FROM
underworldamusements.com

Index

"Achbold" (sensible citizen), 12
Anderson, George W., 81
Aristophanes, 24

Baruch, Bernard, 28, 47
"Battling Baker" (boxer), 70
Bodenheim, Maxwell, 102
Bohrod, Aaron, 99
Brundage, Slim, 105
Burleson, Albert Sydney, 82

Chicago
    Art Institute of Chicago, 99
    Augustana Hospital, 94
    Belmont Avenue, 96, 98
    Blackstone Hotel, 32
    Brewster, The, 102
    Chestnut Street, 96, 105
    Chicago Armory, 102
    Chicago Avenue, 62, 85
    Clark Street, 96, 98, 105
    Congress Hotel, 45, 47
    Contemporary Art Museum, 102
    Coq de la Rue, 105
    Dearborn, 96
    Dearborn Street, 96, 105
    Dil Pickle Club, 76, 83, 103, 105
    Dill Pickle Club, 84
    Diversey Parkway, 102
    Division, 96
    Front Porch, The, 105
    Halsted Street, 98
    House of Blazes, 61
    Irving, The, 98
    Lake Michigan, 61
    Le Bistro, 105
    Lincoln Avenue, 94
    Lincoln Park, 64
    Locust, 96
    Medinah Temple, 26
    Newberry Library, 23, 92, 93, 99, 101, 102
    Newberry Park, 35, 36
    North Clark Street, 23, 62
    Oak Street, 96, 98
    Pizen Pup Kafe, 83
    Pompeii Inn, 85
    Post Office, 12
    Radical Book Shop, 62
    Roué, The, 105
    Rush Street, 85, 105
    Saddle Club, 103
    Sheridan Road, 23
    State Street, 96, 98, 105
    Toguri Mercantile, 96
    Tooker Alley, 83, 105
    Top Hat Lounge, 103
    Trotzky Square, 62
    Washington Square Park, 23, 83, 103
    Webster Street, 94
    William B. Ogden School, 96
    Windsor Theatre, 96
Chicago Avenue, 84
Chicago Daily News, 52
Christ, Jesus, 20, 42, 63
Christensen, Parley P., 62
Clabaugh, Hinton C., 79
Cotney, Florence, 83, 84
Cox, James M., 61, 62, 64, 71

Daley, Richard J., 92, 105
Debs, Eugene, 27, 51, 62

Fallows, Samuel, 76
Field II, Marshall, 70, 71
Fitzpatrick, John, 32

"Foch" (of Khartoum), 43
Ford, Henry, 76
"Foster" (IWW), 27

Garfield, Harry A., 51–53
Gary, Elbert Henry, 59
Goldman, Emma, 102
Gompers, Samuel, 81
Greenwich Village, 84

Hansen, Will, 92
Harding, Warren G., 61–64, 71, 73
Haslett, Duke, 105
Haywood, Bill, 27
Hirt, Adolph (Mrs.), 10
Hohenzollern (family), 11
Holy Mary, 103
Hoover, Herbert, 61
Hus, Jan, 71

Industrial Workers of the World, 15, 24, 27, 30, 32, 38, 41, 48, 53, 54, 61, 64, 80, 105

Jacob, Lawrence, 84
Johnson, Hiram, 47
Jones, Jack, 76, 84

King of the Hoboes, 103
Kitchener, Herbert, 43

Lane, Franklin K., 80, 81
Lavallé, Sidonie, 93
Lenin, Vladimir, 23, 54
Lewold, Tula C., 82
Lincoln, Abraham, 41, 43
Lodge, Henry Cabot, 47, 79

Maury, Vernon, 105
McAdoo, William G., 51, 59, 61–63
Michiewicz, Adam, 10
Mickeqicz, Slowacki, 10
Miller, D. Isaak, 76
"Mitchie" (to apprehend QVB), 81
Morgan, J. P., 12, 28, 29, 41

Newberry Library, 89

Noga, Adolph, 94, 96, 98
Noga, Anthony, 94
Noga, Daniel, 91, 92, 94, 97, 98
Noga, Flora, 92, 99, 103
Noga, Francois, 103
Noga, François, 91, 93, 96–99, 102
Noga, Jozeph, 94, 98, 99
Noga, Kathleen, 92, 96, 101
North Clark Street, 84
North LaSalle Street, 84

Palmer, A. Mitchell, 51, 65, 79
Palmer, Andy Kid, 70
Palmer, John M., 15
"Patten" (sensible citizen), 12
Paul, Alice, 65
Pershing, Josh J., 31, 43
Pizen Pup Kafe, 84

Rapsutin, 54
Reynolds, Wellington J., 99
Robins, Raymond, 20
Roosevelt, Theodore, 10, 47, 70
Rosenwald, Julius, 42, 47
Rotschield, 42, 43, 45, 46

Savonarola, Girolamo, 71
Schwab, Charles M., 28, 29
Scully, Thomas F., 10
"Simms" (IWW), 27
Sinatra, Frank, 105
Sinkiewicz, Henryk, 10
"Spanish" Mary, 105
St. Paul, 24
Strabo, 24
Szukalski, Stanisław, 103

Taft, William H., 74
Toguri, Iva, 96

Washington, George, 25, 41
Wilhelm II, 51
Wilson, Woodrow, 28, 31, 43, 46–48, 51, 59, 66, 69, 71, 79, 81
Wood, grant, 99
Wood, Leonard, 27, 31, 32, 51, 60, 62, 70, 71

www.ingramcontent.com/pod-product-compliance
Lightning Source LLC
Chambersburg PA
CBHW070149080526
44586CB00015B/1910